Y0-BED-555

THE GIFT OF DREAMS
A CHRISTIAN VIEW

Kathryn Lindskoog

Published in San Francisco by
HARPER & ROW, PUBLISHERS
New York, Hagerstown, San Francisco, London

For Anna Katherine Turecek and Julie Marie Pinnix

So young a child ought to know which way she's going, even if she doesn't know her own name.

Lewis Carroll, *Through the Looking-Glass*

THE GIFT OF DREAMS: A Christian View. Copyright © 1979 by Kathryn Lindskoog. All rights reserved. Printed in the United States of America. No part of this book may be used or reproduced in any manner whatsoever without written permission except in the case of brief quotations embodied in critical articles and reviews. For information address Harper & Row, Publishers, Inc., 10 East 53rd Street, New York, NY 10022. Published simultaneously in Canada by Fitzhenry & Whiteside Limited, Toronto.

FIRST EDITION

Designed by Patricia Girvin Dunbar

Library of Congress Cataloging in Publication Data

Lindskoog, Kathryn.
    The gift of dreams.

    Bibliography
    Includes index.
    1. Dreams.   I.   Title.
BF1078.L53   1979   248'.2   78-19504
ISBN 0-06-065248-9

79 8 81 82 83   10 9 8 7 6 5 4 3 2 1

CONTENTS

PREFACE

"What's in it?" said the Queen.
"I haven't opened it yet," said the White Rabbit;
"but it seems to be a letter, written . . . to somebody."
"It must have been that," said the King, "unless it
was written to nobody, which isn't usual, you
know."

Lewis Carroll, *Alice's Adventures in*
Wonderland

This book is a letter written to all who are interested in their
dreams, to all who are interested in becoming interested in their
dreams, and to all who are interested in other people who are
interested in dreams.

My friend Marilyn Peppin led me into my own dream life years
ago. My husband John has helped me immeasurably with his
research, background study, practical encouragement, patience,
insight, and wit. I thought he should sign as co-author, but he

v

declined because he didn't write the book. To tell the truth, he didn't even read it until a few days after it was finished.

The day I finished this book I dreamed that John had just read it and was giving me a lengthy critique. One phrase he used shocked me so deeply that I awakened in horrified despair.

"The entire book," he declared with finality, "is *sickeningly whimsical.*" First read, first reviewed, and first condemned in a nightmare. Some debut for a serious book all about the value of dreams.

As soon as I was awake enough to realize what had happened, I knew that this dream spoof was itself the ultimate in whimsy. I like a joke like that. It was an appropriate gift that came at just the right time. I think all dreams are gifts.

THE DISGRACE
OF DREAMING:
CLOSED MINDS

"If there's no meaning in it," said the King, "that saves a world of trouble, you know, as we needn't try to find any."

Lewis Carroll, *Alice's Adventures in Wonderland*

A World of Trouble or Illusion

A stranger in a business suit asked me what I was writing about now, and I answered politely, "The meaning of dreams."

"Ha!" he scoffed loudly. "Dreams don't mean *anything*!"

"Speak for yourself," I thought, and I woke up. That was the end of *him*. A truly perfect squelch.

But I still remember him and find meaning in him, which illustrates that he was not only rude but wrong.

Furthermore, I think it was all a good-natured joke in the first place. How preposterous for a figure in my dream life to try to tell

1

me that dreams can't tell me anything. I'll be the judge of that. If this dream told me nothing else, it told me that I'm not into this profound and serious subject without a generous grain of salt and a dash of humor.

The stranger with the suit was making a charge against me and my belief in the value of dreams. Most likely his suit not only represented his sensible conformity to what is proper but also was a reminder that all the people whose opinion he represents make a case, a kind of suit, against dreams. Those of us who believe in the goodness of dreams stand accused in the court of public opinion. Our accusors include many outstanding people throughout history, from several hundred years B.C. to today.

The author of Ecclesiastes declared poetically:

For a dream comes with much business,
    and a fool's voice with many words. . . .
For when dreams increase,
    empty words grow many. . . . (Ecclesiastes 5:3,7, RSV)

Some Chinese sage put it this way: "To believe in one's dreams is to spend all one's life asleep."

In Greece about four hundred years before Christ Plato wrote that the most evil type of man is the one who, in his waking hours, lives out the urges expressed in his dreams. Plato was concerned about the immorality of dreams:

In sleep, when the rest of the soul, the rational, gentle and dominant part, slumbers, the beastly and savage part, replete with food and wine, gambols and, repelling sleep, endeavors to sally forth and satisfy its own instincts. . . . There is nothing it will not venture to undertake as being released from all sense of shame and all reason. It does not shrink from attempting to lie with a mother in fancy or with anyone else, man, god, or brute. It is ready for any foul deed of blood. . . . There exists in every one of us, even in some reputed most respectable, a terrible, fierce and lawless brood of desires, which it seems are revealed in our sleep."[1]

Plato and Aristotle both believed that dreams are caused mainly by physical conditions that disturb sleepers, such as tangled bedclothes. Aristotle figured that there are three explanations for dreams that seem to come true. First, dreamers can sometimes guess ahead correctly about illnesses that are beginning in their bodies. Second, people will do things later just because they dreamed that they did them; then prophecy is self-fulfilling. Third, a few dreams are bound to come true by sheer coincidence because there are so many of them.[2]

Aristotle couldn't have guessed how many dreams there really are. Until recently everyone greatly underestimated the number. The average person has at least a thousand major dreams in a year, not counting an untold number of dream fragments and vague or dull dreams. Only a tiny fraction of these are ever recalled in waking life. The numbers alone seem to support the idea that dreams are worthless.

If only one person in four recalls just one dream on a given day, that means that 1 billion dreams are recalled around the world that day. At that rate in one year there are 20 billion dreams recalled in the United States and 365 billion in the world.

That there are so many potentially meaningful dreams recalled by the people of the world does seem incredible. And the idea that every night 3 billion people fail to retain even one of their several meaningful dreams sounds too unreasonable to consider. Nature is profligate, we know, but it is hard to imagine countless billions of really worthwhile dreams being created and forgotten all the time. Any gift that cheap can hardly be of value.

The Greeks were quite interested in dreams in spite of Plato's and Aristotle's view. That is probably why the faithful Jew Joshua ben Sira came out strongly against dreams about 190 B.C. when he saw Greek culture threatening to take over Palestine. He was urging Jews to live like good Jews. Ben Sira's book of wisdom, now called Ecclesiasticus has never been accepted as Holy Scripture by the Jews or Protestants, but it is accepted by the Roman Catholic church.

Ben Sira says loudly, "Dreams don't mean *anything*!" But he says it in style:

Vain and deceptive hopes are for the foolish,
    and dreams put fools in a flutter.
As well clutch at shadows and chase the wind
    as put any faith in dreams.
Mirror and dream are similar things;
    confronting a face, the reflection of that face.

What can be cleansed by uncleanness,
   what can be verified by falsehood?
Divinations, auguries and dreams are nonsense,
   like the delirious fancies of a pregnant woman.
Unless sent as emissaries from the Most High,
   do not give them a thought;
for dreams have led many astray,
   and those building their hopes on them have been disappointed.
Fulfilling the Law requires no such falsehood,
   and wisdom is most perfectly expressed by truthful lips.
      Ecclesiasticus 34: 1–8, Jerusalem Bible

Ben Sira had hedged when he said not to give a thought to dreams except those sent from God. But Marcus Tullius Cicero, the great Roman orator and philosopher, stated the case against dreams more completely. He sought to show why God, of all people, couldn't be bothered with human dreams. (Cicero wrote this about fifty years before the dreams that attended the birth of Jesus.)

How few people attend to dreams, or understand them, or remember them. How many, on the other hand, despise them, and think any superstitious observation of them a sign of a weak imbecile mind!

Why then should God take the trouble to consult the interest of this man, or to warn that one by dreams, when he knows that they do not only not think them worth attending to, but they do not even condescend to remember them. For a god cannot be ignorant of the sentiments of every man, and it is unworthy of a god to do anything in vain, or without a cause; nay, that would be unworthy of even a wise man. If, therefore, dreams are for the most part disregarded, or despised, either God is ignorant of that being the fact, or employs the intimation of dreams in vain. Neither of these suppositions can properly apply to God, and therefore it must be confessed, that God gives men no intimations by means of dreams. . . .

If, then, dreams do not come from God, and if there are no objects in nature with which they have a necessary sympathy and connection, and if it is impossible by experiments and observations to arrive at a sure interpretation of them, the consequence is that dreams are not entitled to any credit or respect whatever.

And this I say with the greatest confidence, since those very persons who experience these dreams cannot by any means understand them, and those persons who pretend to interpret them do so by conjecture, not by demonstration.[3]

Cicero once dreamed of a ghost who told him a prophecy that later came true in detail. Because he was positive that dreams were utter nonsense, he decided that he had been visited in his sleep by a real ghost rather than a dream ghost.

If the stranger in my dream had been wearing a Roman toga instead of a business suit, I would have guessed that he was Cicero come to taunt me, a dream ghost. "Dreams are not entitled to any credit," Cicero said. The Spanish say, "*De los sueños no creas, ni malos, ni buenos*"—give no credit to dreams, whether bad or good.

Strange Bedfellows

No credit is one thing; bad credit is another. The idea that God doesn't speak in dreams is one reason for ignoring them, but the other side of that coin can serve as a stronger reason. Both Luther and Calvin feared that demons could influence them through their dreams. Luther asked God not to reveal himself to him in dreams at all. Luther trusted his own spiritual discernment in waking life very much and wanted God to reveal himself there, but he felt that his spiritual discernment in his dream life was not sufficient to keep him from being tricked by demons. Once in his waking life Luther hurled a bottle of ink across the room at a devil he perceived there. A symbolic gesture, of course, but a powerful one. Luther preferred to keep such encounters on home ground.

Jeremy Taylor agreed. He has been called "the Shakespeare of the pulpit" because his sermons were so beautiful. He lived at just the right time to be among the first to use the King James Bible when he preached. It was about 1650 when he warned Christians, "If you suffer impressions to be made upon you by dreams, the devil hath the reins in his own hand and can tempt you by that, which will abuse you, when you can make no resistance."[4] He scorned dreams because they are without rule and without reason.

Thomas Hobbes, who lived in England at the same time as Bishop Jeremy Taylor, agreed that dreams are unreasonable:

"Waking, I often observe the absurdity of dreams, and never dream of the absurdity of my waking thoughts."[5]

Unlike Luther and Taylor, Hobbes was hardly worried about the devil; he was sometimes accused of being an atheist and was never quite cleared of the charge. His own father had been a free-wheeling priest who fled to London one day after a brawl in front of his church, leaving his son to be raised by relatives. Hobbes turned out to be a genius and ended up as something of a British institution. He lived through the beheading of Charles I, the rule of Cromwell, the Great Plague, the Fire of London, and repeated controversies and dangers, and was still playing tennis at seventy-four. He was a tutor, traveler, philosopher, scientific thinker, and author.

Although he did not learn geometry until he was forty, Hobbes became almost obsessed with it; he wanted to apply the nature of geometry to politics. He liked to do mathematics in bed, drawing lines on his thighs and sheets, and multiplying and dividing. He was once chosen to teach mathematics to the future King Charles II when they were both in exile. He tried, but he couldn't do it.

Hobbes tried to work out a logical mechanical explanation of almost everything, including dreaming. Because anger heats some parts of the body in waking life, he reasoned, a similar heating in sleep can cause the brain to experience anger and produce a picture of an enemy. Hobbes claimed, erroneously, that there is no sense of time in dreams and that nothing appears surprising or absurd in them. He certainly did not consider dreams at all meaningful. The father of modern analytic philosophy, Hobbes called all human life "nasty, brutish and short," and then lived to be ninety-one. He attributed his own long life to the fact that he made it a point to sing loudly in bed at night.

In the 1700s Daniel Defoe, the Christian author of *Robinson Crusoe*, conjectured about whether giving in to temptation in a dream makes a person as guilty as sinning awake or not. (Many people worry about that.) Across the Atlantic bustling Benjamin Franklin added to his Wise Sayings, "Up, sluggard, and waste not life; in the Grave will be sleeping enough." It seems that if people don't feel guilty about sinning in their dreams, they at least feel guilty about spending so much time in bed with them. It has been claimed that American men lie more about how few hours they sleep than about almost any other subject. Sleeping long hours and paying attention to dreams have both been considered rather unmanly activities in this society.

Alfred Adler, the early twentieth-century psychoanalyst who specialized in inferiority complexes, contributed to the proliferation of his specialty among dreamers when he declared, "Very courageous people dream rarely, for they deal adequately with their situation in the daytime."[6] Adler did not know that we all dream regularly, and his assumption that dreaming is a sign of waking incompetence gave people who don't recall their dreams one more reason for reporting with no small satisfaction that they don't dream at all.

Before Adler some theorists attributed dreams to worse flaws than inability to cope with life courageously in the daytime. Binz declared in 1878 in *Überden Traum*, "Every observed fact forces us to conclude that dreams must be characterized as *somatic* [physical] processes, which are in every case useless and in many cases positively pathological."[7]

No wonder that many dreamers were content with the theory that our dreams are the normal result of random stimulation of the retina of the eye, which we imagine into pictures in our sleep. Dr. George Trumbull Ladd, turn-of-the-century psychologist and philosopher, used to awaken himself after a few moments of dozing in order to analyze the patterns of light and dark in his eyes to check on how they had formed his dreaming images. He was sure of his theory, but he never could figure out how these simple patterns could be transformed into complex lines of clear print that some people read in their dreams. Apparently it never occurred to him to wonder how blind people manage to dream as much as others even if their retinas are destroyed. The French philosopher Henri Bergson, who won the Nobel Prize for Literature in 1927, also believed in the "optical" origin of dreams.

Physical origin of the dream process does not say anything one way or the other about the usefulness of the dreams that result from it. But many people assume that a physical origin in the electrical activity of the brain supports the idea that dreams are not informative. Nobel Prize winner Sir J. P. Medawar, a contemporary medical researcher, contends that dream content can be utterly useless. "There should be no need to emphasize," he said, "in this century of radio sets and electronic devices, that many dreams may be assemblages of thought-elements that convey no information whatsoever."[8] Presumably he meant that dreams can be as stupid as some television and radio drivel. Anything is possible.

Dr. Jule Eisenbud, Associate Clinical Professor of Psychiatry at the University of Colorado, has used his sharp wit to puncture inflated accounts of the role of dreams in creativity and accomplishments. He claims that the instances in which people utilize sleep and dreams to achieve constructive solutions to problems are so rare as to be retold again and again, from one textbook to another. "Most people, on the contrary, get up bleary-eyed, irritable, and in need of stimulants of one sort or another to enable them to bear the light of day," Eisenbud observes. Far from spending the night engaged in creatively facing the future, he says, they have spent the night going from one dreary dream to another, "trying to weasel out of conflict-fraught situations by using the most regressively magical devices of Walter Mitty fantasy, the so-called wish fulfillment."[9]

As if it were't enough to have to bear the disdain and suspicion of fine people from Cicero to Eisenbud, dreamers who naturally value their dreams have a new problem today. After the rush for altered states of consciousness in the 1960s the public gradually became more interested in the oldest, most universal altered state of consciousness there is. In the 1970s dreams-without-drugs became something of a fad.

Dozens of dream laboratories speckle the country. Dream study has exploded. Dream discussion groups meet regularly. Dream books cluster on the shelves. Dream articles pop up in magazines and journals more than ever before. Students flock to dream classes in colleges and universities. Dream experts and dream educators tour the radio and television circuit and pontificate from local podiums. There are dream clinics. One certified psychological therapy center in Los Angeles now offers to the public personal dream-quality rating, dream lectures, dream retreats, dream workshops and seminars, dream group training, dream theory books, and dream therapy by mail.

We are repeatedly told that the latest dream method is "one of the most important psychological discoveries ever made." We are told that dreaming aright can bring the world peace, prosperity, and wishes come true. We are also told that most of what we are being told about dreams is false. Book stores are selling a spiral dream diary that consists of little besides blank pages for recording sixty-seven dreams, and eager shoppers have been paying five dollars for them. As if the search for the perfect orgasm in waking life were not enough, readers are urged to achieve more and better orgasms in their dreams. Dreams are occasionally related to astrology, reincarnation, the *I Ching,* auras, fasting, Yoga, out-of-body experiences, spiritism, Tarot cards, mandalas, and numerology, not to mention the traditional cheese-and-pickles connection.

Through the fat years and the lean[10] one thing stays constant. Whether we like it or not, recall it or not, admit it or not, we keep right on dreaming. Most of us dream at least a quarter of our lives away. God made us that way.

False Alarms and True Friends

In spite of what Cicero said about weak imbecile minds, I like to observe my dreams. I will share a personal one here to show why. One morning in May 1978 I awoke from a nightmare. When I had calmed enough to think clearly, I wrote it down. At the top of the page I wrote "A Sinking Feeling," because I was overwhelmed with that sensation. Then I wrote the dream story.

My husband and I were going to a pot-luck dinner at Forest Home Christian Conference Center in the San Bernardino Mountains fifty miles from our home. I had prepared two simple but delicious cheesecakes (I have no such recipe) and sealed them in nice plastic containers for the trip. They were on the kitchen counter ready to go.

In the next scene we had arrived at our destination an hour or two later and went around to get the desserts from the back of the car. There I found two nice containers that held only old food scraps from my refrigerator. My cheesecakes were at home on the kitchen counter! All I had was ugly leftovers to take in to the dinner. I awoke in anguish, with my heart pounding wildly, as if all had been lost forever.

Forest Home had certainly been on my mind before I had that dream, because I was scheduled to give a banquet address there in June at the end of the seventh annual Forest Home School of Christian Writing. When I told my husband about the nightmare later that day, he answered knowingly, with a twinkle, "So what did you use for your after-dinner speech?"

"Nothing," I answered. "I woke up in a panic." I agreed with his interpretation. I was indeed extra careful to take my speech with me.

At the banquet we sat with Norman and Virginia Rohrer and Sherwood and Winola Wirt, who led the writing school. Norman asked me what my current projects were, and I mentioned a future book about dreaming.

"In fact," I said, "I had a nightmare recently about this very dinner. I dreamed I was to bring part of the dessert and I accidentally left it at home. But I brought my after-dinner speech here safe and sound, so the dream didn't come true."

A bit later the waitress approached our table apologetically. "You were supposed to get cheesecake for dessert tonight," she said, "but for some reason we don't have enough to go around. You can have some plain white cake or a dish of Jello instead."

"That was the very cheesecake I left at home!" I muttered to Norman. I looked at the pieces of cheesecake on a neighboring table, and they did look exactly like what I had made in my dream. The entire evening was a delight, and I chuckled about the nightmare as we walked to our car in the fragrant mountain air to head homeward under the brilliant stars.

Many weeks later I came across the piece of paper with that dream written on it. I had a hunch that there was more to it than the speech and the missing dessert. I decided to explore it a minute or two to see if anything more would come of it.

"What do the key items in the dream suggest to you?" is one of the first questions that many people use when checking for a meaning. I recalled an old motto that Forest Home had used: "One mile closer to heaven." (It is about one mile above sea level, in Forest Falls, where I have enjoyed many short hikes in the past. I am a nature lover.)

What do two cheesecakes mean to me? The best of desserts. I suddenly remembered that, long before I discovered real cheesecake, I learned the word as a child during World War II, when it referred to pretty legs that soldiers admired. At least that is how I understood it. In my dream I first had a nice pair of matching cheesecakes. Legs! It clicked. With this silly pun the dream was coming into focus.

Just before my dream about cheesecake I had had a few speaking engagements in which I had difficult stairs to navigate unaided or no lectern to use for steadying myself during my speech. Because I have multiple sclerosis this was a real strain. My balance is off, and my strength and coordination vary from hour to hour. Fortunately, I can walk without any aids, but I have to walk somewhat slowly and carefully rather than gliding along. I can't walk a mile anymore. I don't know if I will ever get used to that, because I was always a quick, light-footed person. Have I left really good legs behind me in the past, and do I find myself with just some old scraps instead? I have to admit that deep inside I feel exactly that way.

The dream dessert had stood for a speech in real life. A speaker often fears "falling on her face" or "failing to get across to people." That is how I feel literally rather than figuratively. The very intensity of the nightmare and the fact that I had labeled it "A Sinking Feeling" showed me that perhaps I should start to pay attention to my mild insecurity about walking and standing in public and my touch of embarassment when I sway or trip.

All the analysis of the dream took only a few minutes. If I had wanted to shrug it off, I could have done that. But I thought it was worth keeping in mind.

A tremendously simple idea floated into my head one day after that. I could make it a point to ask anyone who is present to walk beside me and let me lean on a helpful arm when I feel weak or wobbly. I could also avoid shoes that aggravate the balance problem. Until now that never quite entered my mind, because I was so busy cheerfully ignoring the problem. Most important, I soon started physical therapy in order to learn about my legs and improve them as much as I can. I'm sure I have the dream to thank for that decision, because previously I had been very reluctant to face physical therapy.

That dreadful lost-dessert dream has served like a friendly arm to help me along the way. My later dream about the stranger who scoffs at dreams was like a friendly arm that gave me a mild poke in the ribs for laughs. Many people think of dreams as humiliating false alarms. I think that they are there to serve as friendly arms if we know how to lean on them.

But before we consider ways to become friendlier with our dreams, let's look at what is going on during the third of our lives that is usually as hidden from us as the dark side of the moon.

Notes

1. Plato, *The Republic*, Book Nine. Plato's view of dreams is discussed by Morton Kelsey in *Dreams: The Dark Speech of the Spirit* (Garden City, New York: Doubleday, 1968), pp. 60–66.
2. Aristotle, *On Divination*. As excerpted in *The New World of Dreams,* edited by Ralph L. Woods and Herbert B. Greenhouse (New York: Macmillan, 1974), pp. 168–171.
3. Cicero, *On Divination,* translated by C. D. Yonge. As excerpted in *The New World of Dreams,* pp. 171–173.
4. Jeremy Taylor, "Sermon 9," *Sermons of Jeremy Taylor.* As excerpted in *The New World Of Dreams,* pp. 162–173.
5. Thomas Hobbes, *Leviathon.* As excerpted in *The New World of Dreams,* p. 177.
6. Richard M. Jones, *The New Psychology of Dreaming* (New York: Grune & Stratton, 1970), p. 78.
7. Sigmund Freud, *The Interpretation of Dreams* (New York: Avon Books, 1965), p. 109. As Norman MacKenzie points out in *Dreams and Dreaming* (New York: Vanguard Press, 1965), pp. 65–67, Freud (who referred to many major and minor dream theorizers) failed to mention the early church father Gregory of Nyssa, whose book *The Making of Man* included passages that presage Freud's theory.
8. Norman Mackenzie, *op. cit.*, p. 11.
9. Montague Ullman and Stanley Krippner, *Dream Telepathy* (New York: Macmillan, 1973), p. 254.
10. Genesis 41.

THE HOUSE
OF DREAMS:
BRAIN MATTER

Sleep faster, we need the pillows.

Yiddish Proverb

The New Discoveries

One of the greatest discoveries in the history of human dreaming happened in April 1952—the discovery of what is sometimes called "rapid sleep." It opened the floodgates to our new understanding of how humans dream. It tells you what you never could have guessed about yourself.

Ironically, the physiology student who made the discovery was not extremely interested in dreams to begin with and did not even believe his discovery at first. He thought his machinery was defective when it reported that sleepers in a laboratory at the University of Chicago went through periods of very active eye movement. When he checked the sleepers in person, however, he could clearly see the eye movement under their lids.

The discovery was revolutionary, because experts had believed that the eyes rest quietly throughout sleep. This theory was so reasonable that ancient accounts and the testimony of Yale professor John Trumbull Ladd in 1892 that the eyes move during sleep had been ignored; the observations of thousands of ordinary people for thousands of years watching their children and spouses and noticing occasional flurries of eye movement during sound sleep were never taken into consideration at all. "Anecdotes" frequently don't get much respect from scientists, and sleeping eyes were pronounced inactive until their movements were proved in a laboratory.

When laboratory tests with electrodes finally recorded the age-old movements on polygraphs, the scientific world gradually got excited. The student who made the discovery, Eugene Aserinsky, went into more traditional fields of physiology. But his director, Nathaniel Kleitman, joined by William C. Dement, continued studying this eye movement and the questions it raised. Since then more than ten thousand volunteers have slept with their heads painlessly wired to machinery, cooperating with researchers across the nation who have made sleep research the major frontier of brain research in our time.

Until 1953 most of our facts about the physical nature of dreaming were wrong. It was commonly taught that even our longest dreams really take place in condensed form in a few seconds.[1] It was dogma that we don't dream in color. (When I was about seven I heard two relatives arguing about whether my dress was blue or green. That night I dreamed that I could change it back and forth from blue to green, which I did repeatedly. The colors were vivid. Later I was told that I had not had that dream because neither blue nor green can appear in a dream. After that I kept my dreams to myself.)

It was always believed that many people never dream at all and that dreamless sleep is more restful. Because of the lovely Christmas carol, many of us believed that Bethlehem lay in a deep and dreamless sleep while silent stars went by. And it was naturally assumed that sleepwalkers walk during their most vivid dreaming.

All of these ideas are exposed as false now, along with the idea that sleepers are "dead to the world" or can "sleep like a log"—unless logs have us fooled and are doing much more than we can tell. But no matter how strict some people are about their waking thoughts and activities, and no matter how much they object to dreaming, they do spend at least a quarter of their life dreaming.

Thanks to the measurement of brainwaves in thousands of sleepers, we now know from outer physical observation what we never knew before about inner sleep experience.

The Dream House

I decided that the easiest way to picture the whole dream process is as a dream house where you spend much of your life. This dream house is, of course, your sleeping brain. Each of the brain's sleep stages is like a special room. Every time you enter the house, you walk briefly across the front porch, which is neither out in the waking world nor fully inside the house of sleep. The technical name for this front porch is *hypnagogic imagery.* If you were to fall back off the porch into the fully waking world, you might marvel, as I used to, at the beauty of gorgeous colored patterns you saw there. They can have texture and depth, like breath taking window displays or works of art or wonders of nature. Sometimes they are ordinary scenes or feelings. They can be mini-dreams. They can be sounds. But usually they are not remembered. I was surprised to learn that my son had noticed them when he was very young and assumed that they came to put him to sleep at night.

Next, you find yourself in the living room, which, as we will see, is indeed the liveliest room in the house. The transition to sleep sometimes causes a *myoclonic jerk* at this point, a body spasm that startles sleepers and may make them think the bed has collapsed. This jerk is natural and harmless. If all goes well, you may spend an uneventful five minutes in the living room and then walk into the family room for ten or fifteen minutes. The difference shows in brain wave patterns. This is a casual room with less specific known purpose than the others.

If you are awakened at this time in the living room or family room, you may believe that you were lying in bed thinking all the time instead of lightly dreaming. But the sleep researchers and their equipment aren't fooled. Once when I was awakened at that stage, I had been dutifully cleaning the top of my desk. The dream was as dull and plotless as could be, but finding myself flat on my back in bed without a dustcloth was quite a surprise. If I had been dreaming about lying in bed, as we sometimes do, I wouldn't have realized I had been asleep at all.

Ordinarily you will walk farther back into the house, into the study, for five or ten minutes. There your heart rate, blood pressure, and temperature will decrease. All this time you will be thinking or puttering around or drifting in reverie; minimal but real cerebration. Finally, after being asleep for over half an hour, you enter the bedroom of your dream house. This is a crucially important room. It is what researchers call Stage IV sleep. It seems like oblivion, but you are still thinking or imagining all the time. This is where sleepwalking and sleeptalking usually take place. Dreams experienced here are rarely recalled.

When you are in the bedroom, you are hard to awaken. It is while you are in the bedroom that your pituitary gland releases its growth hormone. Children, appropriately, make superb use of this room. They seem so sound asleep while they are dreaming in the bedroom that they can wet their beds or slip into night terrors or be moved about without realizing it.

When people are deprived of sleep in experiments or "waka-thons" or catastrophic situations such as war, their catch-up sleep later centers in the bedroom in particular. This bedroom is for the healing of physical weariness. If experimenters purposely awaken people every time they enter the bedroom stage of sleep, after a few nights those people will complain of depression and apathy, although they are getting enough hours of sleep. People with low thyroid levels are unable to get much dream-bedroom sleep because of their hormone problem. That doubles their reason for fatigue.

Unfortunately, once we pass thirty we gradually lose our access to this restorative and energizing place where children live so much. Elderly people who complain that they can't get a good night's sleep anymore are probably complaining because they can't get into their dream bedrooms. It is a great loss.

Stress can temporarily eliminate valuable bedroom sleep for anyone, and depressed people sometimes lack it altogether. Whether the depression causes this sleep problem or the sleep problem causes depression is an open question. Hormones regulate sleep, and sleep regulates hormones.

On a typical night you may spend half an hour in the bedroom on your first visit, then return to the study for fifteen minutes, and then move on into the family room for fifteen minutes. Here you are in a lighter stage of sleep and dream again. Next, a very exciting thing happens to your body. After perhaps ninety minutes you are back at your living room. It has become electrified while you were out. You are in for a jolt. You have been experiencing what I call cool dreams; now you are going to have what I call a hot dream.

When you enter the living room this time, your eyes, which have been resting in any direction until now, suddenly coordinate with each other and begin moving rapidly back and forth or up and down. Your brain literally heats up, and your brainwaves become as fast as if you were concentrating upon something very challenging. If you are a male of almost any age, you have a penile erection, although you probably don't feel sexually aroused. Your breath and pulse become irregular, and massive electrical impulses shoot from the base of your brain to the front. This room is supercharged.

Ironically, in all this excitement your body goes absolutely limp. Your chin sags and your skeletal muscles won't move. If you are awakened too quickly, you may feel paralyzed at first. This condition may well account for the terrifying total paralysis that some people experience in frightening dreams when they try to run or cry out and cannot stir or make a sound.

This is the room where you have your most detailed and dramatic dreams. But usually you stay there only a few minutes during your first excitement before retreating to the relative calm of your family room. Once again you make your way back to the bedroom. But on your second visit to the bedroom you stay a shorter time and move slowly back toward the living room again.

Once again your muscles become flaccid and your interior goes into a flurry of activity, and you dream more complex dreams. This time you might stay ten or twenty minutes in the living room before treking back through the family room and study for another, briefer, visit to the bedroom.

So you spend your night returning, on the average, every ninety minutes to your amazing electric living room. You repeat the trip four or five times. Early in your night's rest you spend more time in the bedroom; as the new day approaches, you spend more time in the living room. Also as the new day approaches, all your dreams are apt to become more vivid and dramatic, but in the living room they also become much longer. All this activity throughout the night has used up only about eight hundred calories.

Normal sleepers who awaken naturally after a night's sleep are most apt to exit from a long living-room dream. Upon rare occasions a sleeper will actually exit from the dream house into the waking world by way of the front porch between sleep and waking, perhaps experiencing there a brief bit of imagery, called *hypnopompic visions*. I have often been awakened by the ringing of my doorbell in the morning, only to discover that the sound was hypnopompic. No one had been on my real front porch at all; the ringing bell had occurred vividly on the front porch of my dream house as I headed out toward the waking world.

Of course, no one knows what is happening while you carry on in wild ways in your dream living room. But normal people who are deprived of living-room sleep become irritable and anxious until they are allowed to do some catching up. People who are learning masses of new matter in their waking lives seem to spend more time in their dream living rooms, and people who are severely mentally retarded or senile rarely go there. Sleep researchers consequently suspect that, among other things, the living-room drama allows the brain to work hard on sorting and storing memories and emotions. Brain organization and repair take place here.

The eye activity, which does not in fact tally with what the dreamer is looking at (as was first thought and is still often said), may well be exercise that sharpens our vision. Blind babies have this movement at first, but it gradually fades away, although blind people dream vividly in their electric living rooms just like everyone else. There seems to be inner-ear movement during dreams also, and we can guess that this movement dwindles away in deaf people, although the subject has not yet been studied.

All mammals that can see have these rapid eye movement periods regularly in their sleep. The only exception is the echidna, a rare little hairy beast that hatches from an egg and then is breast fed. Both it and its cousin, the famous duck-billed platypus, are very special mammals called nontherians. The platypus probably lacks rapid eye movement also, but no one has been able to get one to sleep in a laboratory to check it out.[2] When the binocular aspect of human vision was tested before and after a night's sleep, it was much improved by morning. This is the function of two eyes working together that helps us to gauge distance by coordinating our eyes smoothly and quickly. Animals that don't have eyes that work together like ours don't waste time on rapid eye movement in their sleep.

The average frequency of rapid eye movement, or REM (pronounced to rhyme with gem), for humans is every ninety minutes; the average frequency for cats is every thirty minutes; for rats, twelve minutes.

New babies spend half their sleep time in their infant living-room dreams, and premature babies spend up to 85 percent of their sleep in that state. It is easy to suspect that infants spend much of their time in the womb that way, practicing for life, developing their brains.

Adults tend to spend 12 percent of their sleep time in their dream bedrooms and 25 percent—perhaps two hours a night—in their dream living rooms.

The dream living room is not an entirely safe place to be. People with angina sometimes wake up from there in a state of pain and fear for their hearts. People with duodenal ulcers sometimes suffer a flood of acid during the excitement. It is likely that nocturnal asthma attacks occur here, and fatal strokes and heart attacks as well. Heart attacks occur most commonly during the hours when sleepers spend the most time in living-room dreams. It is possibile that the unexplained "crib-death syndrome" of infants is tied to this part of the sleep cycle. We don't know very much yet.

Depressed people are apt to spend much more or much less time in their dream living rooms than healthy people do, and their nightly movements from room to room can be hasty and irregular instead of leisurely and rhythmical. Their body-time is confused.

People suffering from the strange condition called *narcolepsy,* who can't help going to sleep anytime anywhere, turn out to be slipping right out of the waking world into living-room dreams all the time. Bursts of electricity shoot through their brains, their eyes move rapidly, and they take brief naps in the wrong times and places. Students with ordinary narcolepsy are not especially conspicuous, because it is often assumed that they stay up too late like many of their peers; teachers with narcolepsy, however, are in serious trouble. So are people whose narcolepsy causes them to fall to the ground in a limp heap every time they doze off.

Many normal people lose much of their needed living-room dream time because they take drugs such as amphetimines, barbiturates, hypnotics, and alcohol. That is part of the harm that even prescribed drugs, such as some tranquilizers, can do; this dream loss can sometimes cause irritability and anxiety or heightened sexual tension and increased appetite. Cats that are deprived of all living-room sleep in laboratories eventually show bizarre sexual behavior, wildness, and obvious hallucinating. Of course, humans are never deprieved of that much living-room sleep in experiments, but when they are deprived temporarily by researchers who awaken them every time they drift into it, they start to enter that active phase automatically the moment they go to sleep. As soon as they are allowed to do so, healthy humans and animals catch up on any lost living-room sleep. This is a problem in drug withdrawal for addicts, because they tend to experience many nightmares while catching up on their living-room dreams; and they often turn back to drugs because they are frightened by excess nightmares which are, in fact, part of the healing process.

It is possible that people suffering oxygen deprivation lose their living-room sleep. Author Letha Scanzoni, who has unusual dream recall and very active dreams, noticed when she was seriously ill at home late in 1978 that her dreams were only silent

series of faces, hour after hour. She had never dreamed so passive-
ly before in her life. In the emergency room of the hospital doctors
found that her blood oxygen was down to 60 percent of normal
due to pneumonia. When she went to sleep there breathing oxygen, she had one of her usual detailed story dreams right away.
It was a long three-part nightmare about her discovering the devil
incarnate, struggling to protect and serve Jews, being savagely
murdered, and witnessing world-wide cataclysm. Through it all
she was trying to prevent an important assassination, lead people
to Christ, and say goodbye to her family. After all that she
dreamed cheerfully that she went down to the hospital parking
lot, trailing oxygen and intra-venous tubes behind her, to play
ball awhile. She had a good recovery.

A key element in living-room dreaming is bursts of metabolic
energy that surge from the *pons* at the back of the brain to the
more advanced centers at the front. These bursts are probably
related to hallucinations. When humans and animals are deprived
of sleep long enough, they begin to hallucinate. Is this a case of
energy from the pons having to be discharged while the subject
is awake?

Schizophrenia, which strikes at least one person in a hundred
and is the ailment of one-tenth of our hospital patients, is an
extremely complex chemical mystery. One of the strangest facts
about this illness is that it apparently imparts to its victims con-
siderable immunity to cancer. Another strange fact is that, when
people with this problem are deprived of their usual living-room
dream time, they don't catch up on that lost time later, as all other
dreamers do. This raises the possibility that schizophrenics
experience bursts of brain energy when they are awake instead of
only in their living-room dreams, where such bursts belong. The
fact that many schizophrenics complain that they are being
zapped by electricity or rays of some kind could reflect their
awareness of unwanted energy shooting through their waking
brains.

The relationship of living-room dreams to schizophrenia is only
a matter of speculation so far. But it suggests that the crazy events
in our dream living rooms may help us toward waking sanity; that
these peculiar night frolics may sharpen our mental vision as well
as our optical vision.

Technical Means Vs. Meaning

Now that scientific dream research based upon brainwaves is a quarter of a century old, it has gained popularity and respectability. It also has an impressive jargon. Living room sleep is officially Stage I; family room, study, and bedroom sleep are Stages II, III, and IV, respectively. Sleep in the living room on the first visit and in the other rooms at any time are officially called S-State, non-REM, or NREM. Electrified living-room sleep has a dozen different technical names: *REM, REMS, REMP, emergent sleep, transitional sleep, rapid sleep, rhombencephalic sleep, pontine sleep, activated sleep, paradoxical sleep, dreaming sleep,* and *D sleep.* Needless to say, the random overlap of these synonymous terms serves to obfuscate even simple statements and discourages readers. The fact that many books and articles still assume that there is no dreaming worthy of the name anywhere except in the electrified living room (with rapid eye movement) adds greatly to the confusion. Early errors die hard.[3]

It seems that materialists who dislike "other-worldly" subjects feel safe in exploring the biology of dreams. So it was that in 1977 a pair of Harvard psychiatrists, J. Alan Hobson and Robert W. McCarley, came up with what was heralded widely as a great break with traditional understanding of dreams.[4] They were not considering the four-thousand-year-old traditional understanding of dreams; they were breaking with the eighty-year-old understanding of dreams that began with Freud and the advent of modern psychoanalysis.

It has long been obvious that the process of dreaming is physiologically based, and the content of dreams is psychological in nature. The Harvard team has purportedly found new data about that fact. Their research with 120 sleeping cats (Hobson and McCarley in no way claim to believe that cats dream) showed that rapid eye movement periods result from electrical impulses that occur automatically in the brain from time to time. This finding, of course, agrees exactly with previous research. The two researchers have speculated that the human brain makes up stories to try to make some sense out of the rapid eye movement and other excitement caused by this electricity. It is thus no wonder that we experience erratic stories and emotions, both of little consequence. They advise psychiatrists not to pay much attention to dream content any more.

In fact, Hobson admits that, according to this new theory, "it is amazing that we dream anything more than a kaleidoscope of images and colors—that we see anything orderly at all."

No one claims that human speech is largely meaningless simply because it depends upon the automatic breathing apparatus and the eating apparatus for its existence. Yet respectable scientific journals as well as popular news magazines hailed this simple, old-fashioned dream debunking as a big step forward, apparently because laboratory research was involved.

Perhaps someday the dreams in the deeper stages of sleep will be related to a great decrease in electrical activity when cats' eyes rest quietly. Then the theory would be that decreased electricity accounts for deep dreams and indicates that they lack meaning. That theory could appear in major periodicals one of these days as another breakthrough.

Although there is probably real value in the actual Harvard study of the brains of sleeping cats, unnewsworthy as it was, exploring the physical aspects of brain activity in no way leads to the conclusion that electrical impulses short-circuit profound meaning. Speaking of bodily processes, Tolstoy said, "Materialists mistake that which limits life for life itself."

Few people claim that because waking thought takes place by means of electricity and chemistry it is nothing but electrical impulses and random results. And the few people who do believe that certainly don't believe that about their own thoughts on the subject. If thought and reason are all illusions caused by electricity, how could any human functioning in that muddle of chemical illusions figure it out?

C. S. Lewis thoroughly trounced this materialistic "scientific" approach to the mind in a sermon called "Transposition," which he preached one Pentecost Sunday. He asserted that physiology can never find anything in thought except twitching of the grey matter. That is all we can expect of physiology. But saying that thought is "nothing but" twitching of grey matter is like saying that poetry is "nothing but" black ink marks on a piece of paper.

Lewis greatly respected facts, but he rejected teachers who see all the facts and none of the meaning in any area of life. This is reductionism. Some people call it "nothing-buttery." It is the essence of materialism, which rules out higher reality.

"There will always be evidence, and every month fresh evidence," Lewis predicted wryly, "to show that religion is only psychological, justice only self-protection, politics only economics, love only lust, and thought itself only cerebral biochemistry." Lewis debunks this kind of foolishness.[5]

The brain's grey matter and its electrical activity is the physical means for dreaming. It is not the dream. No one knows exactly what the dream is. We don't begin to understand the physical brain yet, much less the mind that works through it.

Notes

1. This common error was presented in a diagram in Emil A Gutheil's *The Language of the Dream* (New York: Macmillan, 1939), p. 4. In the recent edition of Gutheil's 1951 *Handbook of Dream Analysis* (New York: Liveright, 1970), p. 17, this misconception is repeated in the first paragraph of the text, which repeats that dreams come only when we doze off or awaken. Gutheil is a respected authority.
2. Truett Allison and Henry Van Twyver, "The Sleep and Dreams of Animals" in *The New World of Dreaming,* edited by Woods and Greenhouse, p. 347. First published in *Natural History,* February 1970.
3. The decision of some psychologists to rule that dreams outside the electrified living room are no longer dreams but mere mentation is an attempt to narrow the definition of the word dream for the first time in history. If successful, this effort will deprive us of the only word in our vocabulary that means all mental activity during sleep. It is far more efficient to invent a technical term for the new concept of REM dreaming rather than to appropriate one of the basic words of the English vocabulary for that special purpose. For information about the reality and prevalence of nonREM or cool dreams read *The Psychology of Sleep* by David Foulkes (New York: Charles Scribners Sons, 1966); *Dream Power* by Ann Faraday (New York: Coward, McCann & Geoghegan, 1972), Chapter 2; and "Morpheus Descending" by Ralph Berger in *Psychology Today* (June 1970, pp. 33–36, 70).
4. "Dream machine: end of a fantasy" in *Science News* (December 17, 1977), p. 405; "What's in a Dream" in *Newsweek* (January 16, 1978), p. 50.
5. C. S. Lewis, "Transposition," *The Weight of Glory,* (Grand Rapids: Eerdmans, 1965), pp. 28–29.

THREE

A MATTER
OF RECORD:
INNER HISTORY

The strongest memory is weaker than the palest ink.

Traditional Proverb

Dream Amnesia

As individuals, people have forgotten thousands of dreams; as a group, people have forgotten thousands of years of dreams.

In *Alice's Adventures in Wonderland* the White Rabbit asked, "Where shall I begin, please your Majesty?"

"Begin at the beginning," the King said, very gravely, "and go on till you come to the end: then stop."

It was easy enough for the White Rabbit to obey the King's instructions. All he had to do was read some verses in Alice's dream, not remember them after Alice woke up. In real life it is immensely difficult for most people to recall dream material from beginning to end.

Even if one recalls a dream upon awakening, it is often lost forever a few minutes later. C. S. Lewis once described "a man coming gradually awake and trying to describe his dreams: as soon as his mind is sufficiently awake for clear description, the thing which was to be described is gone."[1]

Common dream amnesia is apparently related to the chemistry of sleep. Dreams do not often get filed in our long-term memory banks for future use unless we recall them upon awakening and then stay awake for at least ten minutes before going back to sleep. Even then the chances are slim. This is a fact of physiology. Today brain researchers are just beginning to solve the mystery of the chemistry of memory.

One contemporary dream authority claims that "lucid dreams," the kind in which the dreamer is aware of dreaming, are easy to recall upon awakening.[2] That is not always true. I have an aunt in her seventies who, over the years, has had occasional lucid dreams in which she knew that she was dreaming and wanted very much to bring the dreams back with her to waking life. She exerts herself greatly to memorize the dream and thinks that she is succeeding. She has always failed. She awakens with the knowledge that she had just memorized every detail of something fascinating in her dream life, but it is lost once again as she awakens.

A dream is a letter you send to yourself. Are our lost letters recorded in the depths of our minds somewhere, or do they remain only in the mind of God?

One night recently I dreamed about this question. In my dream my wise friend Thora came to see me. She said that she had asked me in a letter which of two desks I would like as a gift and that I had failed to answer; she came to hear my decision.

"Oh dear," I said, "I completely forgot the contents of that letter as soon as I read it, and I know I can never find it again in the heaps of papers in my study. I can't answer you about the desks."

"That's all right," Thora said. "I keep a file of all our letters." She handed me a folder with copies of all our letters to each other in it so that I could recover her lost message to me. That surprised me, but what surprised me even more was the fact that in her file she even included a note that I had once written to her and then torn up and thrown away! Nothing at all escapes her notice, I realized, and nothing gets lost.

"Isn't that just like Thora," I thought with admiration. "She is always so efficiently at work behind the scenes. She is a genius."

That was the end of the dream. I woke up feeling good.

Whether it is true or not, it is nice to think that I might have an inner Thora not only sending me dreams but keeping track of my responses and filing everything.

In real life Thora has a degree in mathematics and excels in everything practical. She is one of the "sanest" people I have ever known, using her keen powers of analysis and energetic good nature to serve others much of the time. Whatever my inner dream correspondent is really like, she is extremely smart to pick out Thora for representing herself to me. That image is the epitome of calmness, dependability, balance, and common sense.

And how did I manage to remember this dream in which my inner Thora told me that none of our communication gets lost? I wrote it down, of course. Otherwise I probably would have lost it. I know from experience that I am like the White King in *Through the Looking Glass*:

"The horror of that moment," the King went on, "I shall never, *never* forget!"

"You will, though," the Queen said, "if you don't make a memorandum of it."

A New Day For Night Thoughts

Today is the most revolutionary, exciting time there ever was for dream catching. This is not merely because researchers are recording thousands of dreams in laboratories where sleepers are awakened to report the business of their fantasies to all-night secretaries. In fact, a New Jersey psychiatrist named Berthold Schwarz has described the difference between home dreams and laboratory dreams as like the difference between a wild animal in its habitat and a forlorn creature caged in a zoo. That is true. For example, the old admonition against discussing sex, politics, and religion in public seems to somewhat inhibit people who know they are dreaming in public. Homes are the happiest dream-hunting grounds.

Today ordinary bedsides can be equipped to help immensely in catching wild dreams on the run. Preparing to collect dreams is a very practical, common-sense matter. Three centuries ago Jeremy Taylor said, "Whatsoever we beg of God, let us also work for it."

Taylor did not want to record and meditate upon his dreams. But people who wanted to to so in his day usually had to be content with what they could remember the morning after. Houses were too cold and dark at night for much dream recording. It is said that Oliver Wendell Holmes once awakened with such an interesting idea that it seemed worth lighting a candle to write it down. He felt around for the large old-style card of matches and broke off the first one and struck it, but it did not light. He tried one match after another, and because not one of them would light, he finally gave up and went back to sleep. No one knows what his lost idea was, but the next morning his upset wife wanted to know who had broken all the teeth off her tortoise-shell comb during the night.

It is frustrating to a literate person to lose an idea because of the dark. Perhaps illiterate people are accustomed to losing ideas because they can't write them down day or night. The Alorese tribe that lives on a small jungle island in Indonesia has used a unique solution to the problem of retaining night dreams. Dreamers are expected to awaken the rest of the household when they have something interesting to share, and the whole family discusses the dream before going back to sleep.

Now almost anyone who is capable of writing dreams on paper can do so at night with a bedside lamp or flashlight. Those hardy sleepers who don't awaken spontaneously during the night and who can, like the Alorese, tolerate interruptions, may set an alarm clock to go off about four hours after they go to sleep. First they must determine to write down whatever they were experiencing or "thinking" at the time. Notebook and pens or pencils must be laid out, all ready. With either an alarm or natural awakenings, it may take quite a few bedtime pep-talks or times of contemplation and several nights of practice before any dreams get written down. A rapid awakening with as little movement as possible is the best way to catch a dream as it bounds away. Get the key phrases, feeling, pictures in mind, and then turn on the light and start writing.

Some people find that open eyelids or light itself instantly erases their dreams. It is better in that case to learn to write with eyes closed in the dark. I suggest a fairly soft pencil for this purpose to guarantee that there will be marks on the paper in the light of day. I developed a simple aid called "Jacob's Ladder" (in memory of Jacob's most famous dream), which, though not guaranteeing good penmanship, guarantees that the lines of scribbling won't end up on top of each other. Cut a piece of very heavy paper into an overlay guide by leaving one-inch margins on each side like the sides of a ladder and then removing many horizontal strips between the two sides. This will leave horizontal "ladder rungs" that will channel your writing across the page underneath. Space the rungs according to the size of your writing. Cutting two or more identical ladders and gluing them together provides desirable thickness.

I suggest a standard clipboard that holds several loose sheets of three-hole paper securely at the top. Clip the Jacob's Ladder guide over this paper, and lay out more than one pencil beside it. Practise on one of the pages with your eyes shut. Mark the line you are writing on with your left thumb or forefinger (if you are right-handed) so that each time you finish a line your left hand can guide your right hand down to the next line. When you are at the bottom of a page, loosen the clip, toss the completed page aside, and go on to the next one under the guide. In the morning you can gather the pages into a three-ring notebook and copy the material as soon as convenient for permanent storage, allowing space for future comments and insights.

I don't write down my dreams any more if I can help it. I have much better success with a tape recorder, because I am extraordinarily incompetent immediately after awakening. Once recently I tried very hard to write down an especially meaningful dream because my tape recorder was not available. The dream gave direct advice about interpreting dreams! When I read the paper after I got up, it said, "At 6:30 Wed Sept a awoke from dreaming This was a good aid for drean interp." That is all that is left of the special dream. That was a perfect example of what to leave out when recording a dream, and so my effort was not completely wasted.

The ideal tool for most people, I am sure, is a cassette tape recorder with an attachable microphone that has an off-on switch in it. The microphone is on a light-weight cord. At night I make sure that the recorder has enough blank tape in it and is all set for recording, with no more buttons or dials to be touched later. (When I awoke one morning and found the forward and backward buttons both jammed in at the same time, I decided that a recorder is too valuable to entrust to my hands when I am half asleep.) All you have to do to record a dream is to lift the microphone to your lips and flip its switch on. I can sleepily whisper my dream into the microphone, with covers pulled over my head if I need to be extra quiet, and I can flip it off and on to save tape if I pause to gather my thoughts.

One advantage of tape recorders is that the experience of monitoring the tape later in the day in order to copy the dreams into a dream diary can be amazing. To hear one's very own voice earnestly telling tales that have been totally erased in memory in the intervening hours is sometimes bewildering, hilarious, or deeply moving.

Early Dream Study

Catching dreams on cassette tape seems almost unsporting when one thinks that for thousands of years many people have had intense interest in their dreams and have had to get along with very little help. All preliterate people, it is said, consider dreams significant—although this significance varies from group to group. It is thought that people have probably been writing about dreams and their meanings almost as long as they have been writing anything. Picture writing began over five thousand years ago, and early Egyptian hieroglyphics evolved around 3000 B.C. The superb Chester Beatty papyrus from about 1350 B.C. lists about two hundred traditional dream interpretations that had probably been written down repeatedly for many centuries before that. It is on view in the British Museum along with other famous exhibits from ancient Egypt.

The Book of the Dead, which was read to the dying in Egypt to help them adjust to the mysteries of the next life, assumed that they would be able to communicate with people in this world through dreams. Development of this book went on from about 1500 B.C. to 500 B.C.

Dreams were extremely important in Sumeria and Babylonia as well as in Egypt. The epic story of Gilgamesh, from about 2000 B.C., tells of both the hero's dreams and his adventures.

Many groups in the ancient Near East and the Orient believed, as some people do today, that in dreams the soul leaves the body and travels abroad. This is the idea fancifully expressed for children in Eugene Field's poem "Wynken, Blynken and Nod," in which the little sleeper goes fishing in the sky for stars while he dreams.

Ancient people believed that important messages could come from gods and spirits in dreams, especially to rulers and heroes, and they sometimes tried to promote desired dreams within themselves or others through prayers or magic. The most noted of these practices was *incubation,* the promotion of healing dreams. Sick people in Egypt, and later in Greece, would sleep in a healing temple in hopes of dreams that would diagnose, prescribe, or cure their ills. This practice also occurred in China around 3500 years ago and still survives in some forms today in various countries. Incubation may have originated in ancient Assyria.

The earliest great library known in history was that of the Assyrian King Ashurbanipal, assembled around 650 B.C. in Ninevah, when that city was at the height of its splendor before its destruction by Babylon. It is believed that among these clay tablets there was dream lore going back thousands of years, some of which comes down to us through one of the truly great figures in the history of dreams—Artemidorus.

Artemidorus was a Roman who wrote the *Oneirocritica* (study of dreams) around 150 A.D. He collected about three thousand dreams. He claimed, "I have done no other by day and night but meditate and spend my spirit in the judgment and interpretation of dreams." He was so successful that when his book was finally translated into English 1500 years later it went through twenty-four editions in less than a century. Most popular dream books since Artemidorus have drawn upon his research of historical traditions and personal observations.

Artemidorus sincerely believed that dreams come to us for our advantage and instruction. He believed that most dreams are concerned with revealing the conditions of a dreamer's mind and body, and that the other, less common, dreams are of a deeper spiritual nature. He noted the significance of dream series. Sometimes, he noticed, dreams represent just the opposite of their surface message. He observed that the meaning of dreams is often tied into wordplay and puns.

It is possible that many of the traditional interpretations of dream matter originated in the lost wordplay and puns of ancient languages now out of use for thousands of years. One interesting visual pun given by Artemidorus is the dream of having one's scalp scratched by an acquaintance; that is apt to signify being "scalped" by the person financially. Some figures of speech, such as "scalped," have come down through thousands of years, from one language to another. Many ideas about dreams have survived the same way.

Artemidorus, unlike many imitators since his time, warned readers that dreams have to be interpreted according to the identity of the dreamer. Symbols are bound to sometimes mean completely different things for different dreamers.

Less than three hundred years after Artemidorus another great dream book, *Concerning Dreams,* was written by Synesius, from Cyrene in North Africa, a brilliant, handsome, talented, wealthy man who converted to Christianity at age thirty-five. Although he was married, he was made a bishop, and he made a good one. He claimed that his writing about dreams was, unlike his other writings, directly inspired by God. His book has never had the influence of that of Artemidorus because it is very difficult. Not only was Synesius interested in traditions and practical interpretation, but he sought to explain the importance of dreams with sophisticated philosophical and psychological insights. His is perhaps the most profound study of dreaming before the twentieth century, añd it seems ironic that it was lost to the West long ago. In Byzantium a commentary to help readers understand Synesius was added a thousand years after he wrote the book.

Synesius urged those who are serious about their dreams to keep a record of them so that they may know their sleeping lives well. He said, "No one is urged to quit his work and go to sleep, especially to have dreams. But as the body cannot resist prolonged night-watches, the time that nature has ordained for us to consecrate to repose brings us, with sleep, an accessory more precious than sleep itself: that natural necessity becomes a source of enjoyment and we do not sleep merely to live, but to learn to live well. . . . "[3]

Because the wisdom of Synesius was lost, it can be said that from Artemidorus to Freud, 150 to 1900 A.D., there were no major gains in the understanding of dreams. People believed this and that. Some wise people puzzled and theorized over dreams, foolish people used foolish dream interpretation books, and the only consensus that evolved was that more scientific, technologically advanced cultures took less interest in dreams.

Before we hurtle into the twentieth century, we shall stop just long enough for three glimpses into the seventeenth century.

The great philosopher René Descartes, when he was still a very gifted young man with no sense of purpose, had a triple dream on the night of November 10, 1619, after a day spent in a stuffy room considering mathematics. Although Descartes believed that all sleepers dream all the time and that dreams are of physical origin and only express wishes, those special dreams of his seemed a divine command that he must devote his inner life to the search for truth by applying the mathematical method to all other studies. Descartes was so shaken that he needed a few days to adjust himself, and then he began to write. After that, it seems, he never quit. It is ironic that he owed his success to a dream in spite of the fact that he opposed serious consideration of dreams.

Morton Kelsey has called Descartes' dream the dream that would eventually put an end to dreaming. Arthur Koestler has referred to it as a catastrophe. Descartes' method of thinking led him to see matter and mind as quite separate, and he identified mind with conscious thinking and rational awareness. Dreams are obviously neither matter nor conscious thinking, and so there was no good place for them in his view of reality. However, like many people before and after him, Descartes thought enough about dreams to remark that he was astonished by the fact that his dreams were convincing to him while he was dreaming and that there is no certain way for a person to ascertain whether he is asleep or awake: ". . . in amazement I almost persuade myself that I am now dreaming. . . ."[4]

Another brilliant French scientist and mathematician whose life overlapped that of Descartes, Blaise Pascal, took that idea a bit farther. We all agree, he reasoned, that no matter how real our sleeping dreams seem to us, they are illusions. How do we know, then, that when we are "awake" we are not really in a different kind of dreaming sleep? Many of us have dreamed that we went to sleep and had a dream within our dream. Perhaps all of this life is a large dream in which we dream about smaller dreams, and we shall finally awaken at death.[5] Pascal was a devout Christian.

Pascal saw truth far differently than Descartes. Descartes' most famous saying is "I think, therefore I am." He tried to understand everything by doubt and logic rather than by experience. Pascal said, "The heart has reasons that reason cannot know" and believed that mystic faith was essential in addition to reason for a full understanding of the meaning of life. When Pascal had his famous conversion experience, he wrote the following record of that experience on parchment and wore it sewed inside his coat for the rest of his life:

FIRE

God of Abraham, God of Isaac, God of Jacob.
Not of philosophers or men of learning.
Certainty, joy, certainty, feeling, sight, joy.
God of Jesus Christ.
My God and your God.
Thy God shall be my God. Truth.
Oblivion of the world and all outside God.
Joy, Joy, tears of Joy.[6]

Pascal's God was the God of dreamers.

In England at this same time Sir Thomas Browne, a great physician, wrote his essay "Of Dreams," counseling his readers that, although dreams are almost always wrong about outward events, they can be a great aid to self-understanding. Dreams are significant because they are so intimate. Furthermore, Browne decided that Aristotle had been mistaken in claiming that dreams never come from supernatural sources. "If there are guardian angels, they may not remain inactive while we sleep," he reasoned, "but may sometimes influence our dreams, and many strange hints, insights, or discoveries, which are so amazing to us, may arise from that source."[7]

Of course it was Descartes, not Pascal or Browne, who become a great influence upon modern thought; he has been called the father of modern philosophy. Before Descartes perceptive people took it for granted that we can have feelings and thoughts without being consciously aware of them. There is a continuum of mental activity from acute awareness to hidden mental functions. St. Augustine, in fact, had referred to his unconscious memories around 400 A.D. as "a spreading, limitless room within me—who can reach its limitless depth?" As Descartes' rationalism came to dominate our thinking, the "unconscious" part of the mind was not completely ignored, but for many it took on a distasteful occult tang. It seemed strange and, if possible, "unnatural." For many people dream interpretation sank to the status of a parlor game or worse.

The Artist of Vienna

Then Sigmund Freud broke into the twentieth century with the publication of his greatest work, *The Interpretation of Dreams,* in late 1899. It offers readers what C. S. Lewis referred to as the bracing and satisfying experience that we receive from certain books of theory, independent of our final agreement or disagreement; vigorous intellectual systems are similar to works of art.[9] Here Lewis is echoing Thomas Mann. A clear new view of life, philosophical or psychological, gives the same aesthetic satisfaction as a work of art. Freud believed that the human mind is an extremely complicated neurological machine and no more. For him mind practically equaled brain. In seeking more success with his patients who suffered hysterical symptoms, he learned and practiced hypnosis, which was anathema in those days, and then dropped it for other forms of suggestion in his desire to ferret out hidden emotional traumas.

Because his patients shared dreams with him, Freud studied almost all the available material on dreams to try to improve his new art of psychoanalysis. He was a thirty-nine-year-old doctor, always prosperous and respected, but frustrated in his career and longing for greatness. One morning in 1895 he had a peculiar dream about a patient of his named Irma, and when he analyzed what the dream meant about his own inner emotions he felt that he had solved the mystery of human dreaming for all time. He titled his dream "Irma's Injection." He traced many elements in the dream to their sources in his waking life. He recognized his defensiveness about not curing Irma completely and his wish that he could blame her remaining problem on another doctor who bothered him.

Five years after his breakthrough dream discovery, Freud had written and published his book about it and wondered, in a letter to a friend, if someday the house in which he dreamed about Irma would bear a marble plaque, inscribed:

In This House, on July 24th, 1895
the Secret of Dreams was Revealed
to Dr. Sigm. Freud[10]

Few people today are such die-hard Fruedians that they would say *the* secret of dreams was revealed to him in 1895, but most people will admit, even if grudgingly, that he was a pioneering genius and that his book on dreams is a landmark in the advancement of knowledge. He convinced the educated people of our day of the overwhelming importance of the inner world to which dreams are the Royal Road. He claimed that dreams are neither foolishness nor prophecy but tools for exploring the deep levels of the human mind where, in his opinion, biology is sometimes mistaken for soul. He wrote concise, pithy, entertaining prose.

Freud taught us that all the parts of a dream can be significant in themselves, that dreams use conflict-laden material, that dreams incorporate information not readily available in waking life, and that dreams are useful in therapy. They are loaded with meaning. Freud, who was a lover of literature and learned English when he was young so he could enjoy Shakespeare and Milton, won over the literary world of his day before he won over his colleagues in medicine. He had developed an art of dream interpretation that he valued for its rationality and scientific accuracy. Today the behaviorist school in particular believes that he was not adequately rational and scientific.

Freud believed the old idea that dreams are really wish fulfillment. He gave the example of his little nineteen-month-old daughter who was denied food all day long because she had vomited in the morning. That night she called out in her sleep, "Anna Fweud, stwawbewwies, wild stwawbewwies, omblet, pudden!"[11] Anna obviously wished for food. Freud believed that her dream kept her from awakening. Freud believed that dreams guard adult sleep for us by disguising our repressed infantile urges, which float up in the night and would shock us awake if they could. These urges are largely incestuous. Freud invented the term *Oedipus complex,* stressing that males naturally desire to possess their mothers sexually and kill their fathers.

Contemporary philosopher Owen Barfield has suggested that it is a shame for people to think that the Oedipus myth is all about sex. He reminds us of another important part of the story, the riddle of the sphinx about human identity, which could have been very useful in dream interpretation if Freud had noticed it. Barfield's view is ultimately religious. Religion, in Freud's view, was at best an illusion based upon the wish for a good father and at worst a neurotic obsession. He believed all religion is harmful in that it interferes with the scientific effort to grasp reality and perpetuates infantile behavior in adults. If Freud is less popular in the second half of this century that is partly because of his antipathy to anything supernatural and his teaching that women are an enigma designed to serve men.

Although I become irritated at some of Freud's beliefs, I had a pleasant surprise while my husband and I were immersed in a short study of his life and work recently. I had a dream on my husband's birthday that was nothing but a ten-word message for him with no images or feeling: "Sigmund Freud wishes you happy things on your natal day." I awakened and told John, and he said thank you. Freud taught emphatically that dreams express wishes, and I have to admit that in this case he proved himself right. My dream did nothing but express Freud's nice wish.

Freud has always aroused the wrath of one group and another. Some therapists today say scornfully that psychoanalysis is an illness that pretends to be a cure. It is true that psychoanalysis did not turn out to be the reasonably prompt cure that Freud first envisioned it to be. But as Freud said at seventy-seven, when his books and those of other Jews were burned in his homeland and he had to flee to England, "At least I have been burned in good company."[12]

In Freud's dream interpretation the genitals or sexual acts are disguised as many common objects, including coats, hats, lizards, guns, knives, ears, ovens, noses, rakes, rooms, groups of rooms, horses, trees, pencils, purses, stairs, gardens, locks, and so on. A contemporary Freudian literary critic has declared in print that the lamp post in C. S. Lewis' *The Lion, the Witch and the Wardrobe* is obviously Lewis' symbol for a penis in Narnia. One reader of Freud has plaintively asked, "I understand that a key in a lock has to be a disguise for the sex act. Does that mean that when I dream about the sex act it has to be a disguise for a key in a lock?"

Freud's method of interpretation can be illustrated by the dream of one of his patients that she dived into the reflection of the moon in a lake. Freud explained that her inner censor was hiding the fact that she was coming out of the water in her dream, not entering it, and the moon was really an anus, where children believe that babies come from. So in a reversed and childishly inaccurate way, she had dreamed of being born. Freud set up the rules for this kind of interpretation, but he also depended greatly upon intuition in individual cases—his intuition. Denial of his interpretations was interpreted as resistance to therapy.

The Poet of Zurich

It was precisely over this point that Freud's favorite young colleague, Carl Gustav Jung, broke with him in 1912. "It was not

Freud's dream, it was mine; and I understood suddenly in a flash what my dream meant."[13] Jung refused to allow his dreams to be violated by Freud's monotonously sexual interpretations. Jung has become the second major dream interpreter of our century. Being unstylishly committed to the paranormal and far more difficult to read than Freud, Carl Jung has not swept the academic world and radically influenced everything from anthropology to contemporary fiction, as Freud did. However, he is one of the most important dream workers in history. He interpreted about eight thousand dreams.

Jung says that dreams are not disguising the truth to guard our sleep. Rather, they often try to tell us the truth: "There are dreams which embody suppressed wishes and fears, but what is there which the dream cannot on occasion embody? Dreams may give expression to ineluctable truths, to philosophical pronouncements, illusions, wild fantasies. . . . anticipations, irrational experiences, even telepathic visions, and heaven knows what besides."[14]

While I was reviewing Jung's work for a few days, having read most of his book *Memories, Dreams and Reflections* long ago, I had an extremely elaborate and colorful dream in the form of a three-act pageant concerning Jung, set in Switzerland. It escaped me as I awakened, but I knew that it had been very complex, teaching me parallels and contrasts in Swiss theology and philosophy and pointing out some errors. In the second act there had been some business about Bullinger's idea being correct to teach to nine-year-olds and the fact that the sixteenth institute was wrong. I felt so sure that Bullinger was real that, when I arose, I looked him up in my encyclopedia. There he was: Heinrich Bullinger, a sixteenth-century leader in Zurich, Switzerland, which was Jung's city. I had never heard of him before that I could recall. I discovered that he was a Christian reformer in Zurich before Calvin took that role in Geneva, and that he eventually joined Calvin and changed some of his views to Calvin's views. Now all I have to do is to look in Calvin's *Institutes* to see if I can locate the error revealed in my dream. My husband reminded me that the Jung Institute is located in Zurich, and I have no doubt that the pageant I saw in my dream was relating Calvin's *Institutes* to the Jung

Institute and Zurich's Bullinger to Zurich's Jung, with all manners of comparisons and contrasts regarding the teachings of those three great Swiss men and, as I recall, a chorus, beautiful costumes, and dramatic renderings. No wonder I woke up tired.

Another night I simply read some of Jung's writings in a book in my dream. He complained that Freud had wanted too much to be an author. Then I saw to my surprise that Jung had written poetry. I read some of his poetic aphorisms set forth on the page. I turned the page and read a rhymed narrative poem in which he told of a drunken man who was driving erratically along a deserted highway. This man heard an announcement on his car radio that a dangerous drunk driver had been sighted. Terror gripped him; he was afraid of being hit by a dangerous drunk driver. In his panic he sped up, completely lost control of his car, and killed himself in a crash. The warning, Jung concluded, had not been about any other driver. It had been telling the man about himself, if only he had realized. That was the end of Jung's poem and my dream.

The message in Jung's poem was clearly what he and many others teach in prose about dreams: they tell us much more about ourselves than about other people. I can't say that that dream told me anything about myself, as it should have done it it were following its own teaching. But I was reminded of the lines of poetry a couple of weeks later when I was reading the excellent book *Jung and the Story of Our Time* by the English-South African author Laurens van der Post.[15] Van der Post claims that one of Jung's books is a resounding poetic statement and lists some poetic aphorisms of Jung's as examples. I don't recall ever looking into van der Post's book before, but of course it is possible. I am happy to say that the next page had no verses about a drunk driver.

Jung might not have completely disdained the radio announcer idea of dreaming that I attributed to him in my dream. He had asked "who was it speaking in me? . . . Who talked of problems far beyond my knowledge?"[16] Jung spoke of an alien guest, of one we do not know who sees us differently from how we see ourselves and speaks in dreams.

Jung maintained that dreams reflect present attitudes and situations not infantile patterns. He taught that series of dreams are more revealing than single dreams, because themes emerge and later dreams can actually explain earlier dreams. He was convinced that some dreams embody *archetypes,* major symbols that come to us ready-made from the unknown past of the human race.

Jung's autobiographical classic, *Memories, Dreams and Reflections,* is the easiest way to get to know the man and his thought. *Dreams, God's Forgotten Language* by John Sanford, an Episcopal priest now in private practice as a Jungian counselor, serves well as an interpretation of Jungian dream analysis for Christian readers. Morton Kelsey, author of *God, Dreams and Revelation,* (formerly published as *Dreams: The Dark Speech of the Spirit*) is another Episcopal priest profoundly influenced by Jung's insights. Kelsey teaches and counsels at the University of Notre Dame.

"If you are writing about dreams as a Christian," a university dream instructor said to me, "you will want to emphasize Carl Jung, because of course he was a Christian." I mumbled something polite and noncommital. Hers is a common assumption because, in contrast to Freud, Jung said he knew God exists.

Owen Barfield has charged that nearly everyone in the West, including those who deny it, considers consciousness the product physical organisms. Barfield specifically included C. G. Jung in that appraisal. In Barfield's opinion the word *collective* in Jung's term *collective unconscious* points to its apparent origin in an immense aggregate of physical organisms rather than a truly transcendent source.

William McNamara, Roman Catholic priest, Carmelite monk, and author, has observed in his essay "Psychology and the Christian Mystical Tradition,"[17] that Jung's prodigious talent and work in psychology is unassailable, but his references to "God" are bound to confuse most people. McNamara quotes author Augustine Leonard, who claims that, from a religious point of view, Jung's mystic psychology is more dangerous than Freud's materialistic psychology: "That which Jung calls religion, that which he honestly believes to be religion, is not religion at all; *even from the empirical point of view.* It appears to be only a very incidental manifestation."[18] The fact that Carl Jung can hardly be considered a believing Christian does not, of course, invalidate his profound psychological insights. *of course*

The Final Void

Until this century the intellectual problem of dreams has been primarily a philosophical problem, a problem of being and knowing. All kinds of philosophers have grappled with the true nature of the dream experience, the nature of dream content, and the nature of the knowledge of those things. In our century dreams are important in the domains of psychology and physiology. But dreams will always shout loud questions about being and knowing, whether philosophy takes an interest or not.

"A dream ceases to be a delusion as soon as we wake. But it does not become a nonentity. It is a real dream; and it also may be instructive," C. S. Lewis wrote in his last book, *Letters to Malcolm.*[19] Lewis's point would have seemed almost undebatable until 1959.

In 1959 a different Malcolm, American philosopher Norman Malcolm, published a book called *Dreaming.*[20] Macmillan's eight-volume *Encyclopedia of Philosophy* (1967) devotes well over half its entry on the history of the philosophy of dreaming to Malcolm's radical new ideas and states that his book is "clearly the most important discussion of the whole topic. . . . any future examination of the problem will have to take his book fully into account."[21]

Malcolm challenges all previous philosophical ideas about dreams and also dismisses the new physiological studies of dreaming as meaningless. Dreams are not experiences, illusions, workings of the imagination, or anything else they were thought to be. Dreams do not even exist unless they are told to other people. It is the telling that exists, because it can be verified.

Malcolm says that dreams can only take place in sound sleep and that people are never aware that they are dreaming in sound sleep. That would make lucid dreams impossible. Furthermore, he says, people can never talk about the fact that they are dreaming while they are dreaming. I have actually conversed at length with a dreamer about her awareness that she was asleep and dreaming while she was dreaming in sound natural sleep. That occurred on February 9, 1954, five years before Malcolm's book was published.[22] I hate to think of what my experience does to Malcolm's rule or what Malcolm's rule does to my experience. Malcolm's opinion of memory is that "not all cases of factual memory are cases in which the remembered fact is a fact about a remembered event or action."[23] Norman Malcolm and his mentor Ludwig Wittgenstein are leading figures in contemporary American philosophy.[24]

The encyclopedia article concludes by observing that many philosophers would still like to say that dreams occur during sleep, but that because of Malcolm there is no longer any clear meaning in such a claim and certainly no clear support for it.[25]

It seems as if modern philosophy has brought us to the epitome of a trend that C. S. Lewis wryly described as ". . . the process that has led us from the living universe where man meets the gods to the final void where almost-nobody discovers his mistakes about almost-nothing."[26]

Fashions in philosophy come and go, but the records show that dreams are always with us.

Notes

1. C. S. Lewis in an unpublished letter to his brother W. H. Lewis, January 17, 1932. Available in the Marion E. Wade Collection at Wheaton College, Wheaton, Illinois.

2. Patricia Garfield, *Creative Dreaming* (New York: Ballantine, 1974), p. 130.

3. Synesius of Cyrene, "Dreams Take the Soul to 'The Superior Region'" as excerpted in Woods and Greenhouse, *op. cit.,* p. 160.

4. Norman MacKenzie, *op. cit.,* p. 81.

5. Norman MacKenzie, *loc. cit.*

6. William McNamara, "Psychology and the Mystical Tradition," in *Transpersonal Psychologies,* edited by Charles T. Tart (New York: Harper & Row, 1975), p. 398.

7. Morton Kelsey, *Dreams: The Dark Speech of the Spirit* (Garden City; New York: Doubleday, 1968), pp. 179–180.

8. Arthur Koestler, *The Act of Creation* (New York: Macmillan, 1964), p. 148.

9. C. S. Lewis, "Preface," in *The Hierarchy of Heaven and Hell* by J. B. S. Haldane (London: Faber and Faber, 1956), p. 11.

10. Sigmund Freud, *The Interpretation of Dreams* (New York: Avon Books, 1965), p. 154.

11. Sigmund Freud, *op. cit.,* p. 163.

12. Louis Untermeyer, *Makers of the Modern World* (New York: Simon and Schuster, 1955), p. 244.

13. Carl Jung, *Man and his Symbols* (Garden City, New York: Doubleday, 1964), p. 57.

14. Stuart Holroyd, *Dream Worlds* (Garden City, New York: Doubleday, 1976), p. 34.

15. Laurens van der Post, *Jung and the Story of Our Time* (New York: Random House, 1975), p. 207.

16. Carl Jung, *Memories, Dreams and Reflections* (New York: Random House, 1961), pp. 14–15.

17. William McNamara, *op. cit.,* p. 393.

18. Augustine Leonard, "Studies on the Phenomenon of Mystical Experience" in *Mystery and Mysticism: A Symposium* (London: Blackfriars Publications, 1956).

19. C. S. Lewis, *Letters to Malcolm* (New York: Harcourt Brace, 1963), p. 80.

20. Norman Malcolm, *Dreaming* (Atlantic Highlands, New Jersey: Humanities Press, 1962). Malcolm bases his reasoning upon Ludwig Wittgenstein's *Philsophical Investigations.*

21. *The Encyclopedia of Philosophy,* edited by Paul Edwards (New York: Macmillan, 1967), Volume 2, pp. 414–417.

22. For details about this experience see Chapter Eight.

23. *The Encyclopedia of Philosophy,* Volume 5, p. 266.

24. Paul B. Holmer, in *C. S. Lewis, the Shape of his Faith and Thought* (New York: Harper & Row, 1976), seeks to convince readers that the thought of C. S. Lewis is very close to the thought of Ludwig Wittgenstein, which would make Lewis and Malcolm highly compatible. They would seem to me to disagree about the nature of dreams.

25. While browsing in O. K. Bouwsma's *Philosophical Essays* (Lincoln: University of Nebraska Press, 1965) I chanced to come across Bouwsma's presidential address delivered before the fifty-fifth annual meeting of the Western Division of the American Philosophical Association in 1957, "On Many Occasions I Have in Sleep Been Deceived" (pp. 149–173). Bouwsma's address concluded with the hint, "This essay is a clear instance of mitigated plagiarism. My hope is that the plagiarism shows through." My guess is that Bouwsma's rollicking, rambling essay (ostensibly about Descartes) is a thinly disguised commentary on Malcolm's *Dreaming.* Bouwsma has been ignored in dream literature; I recommend his essay heartily for enjoyment and possible refutation.

26. C. S. Lewis, "Preface," in *The Hierachy of Heaven and Hell* by Haldane, p. 11.

DREAMING THROUGH THE BIBLE: A GLAD COMMENTARY

I sleep, but my heart is awake.

The Song of Solomon 5:2, Jerusalem Bible

Bones of Contention

Thomas Paine thought the Bible was a terrible book, and he thought that one of the worst things in it was its dreams. Paine had grown up in a strict Quaker home. The name Paine is from the old Saxon word for pagan. Paine turned out to be part Quaker and part pagan. He never stopped trying to change people and to improve things. He had some success. His prorevolutionary *Common Sense* was the immediate best-seller in 1776, and his further writings helped to carry America to independence.

Paine not only wanted to shape political history, but he also wanted to design beautiful bridges and to reshape religious beliefs. He wanted to free people from superstition. He purposely waited until late in life to begin his spitfire attack upon Christianity and Judaism with his famous book *The Age of Reason: Being an Investigation of True and Fabulous Theology.*

Paine's rational, deistic beliefs were the same as those of Washington, Franklin, and Jefferson, but those men wisely kept their disbelief in the Bible more to themselves. Paine was too much of a fiery reformer to do that. In England the publisher of the first two parts of *The Age of Reason* was prosecuted and found guilty of blasphemy, although the book clearly opposed atheism and immorality. Today *The Age of Reason* stands a few inches from books by C. S. Lewis in the religion section of my public library. If Paine and Lewis had lived at the same time, they could have had grand debates.

When Paine was sixty-nine he published "Essay on Dreams" as the preface to part three of *The Age of Reason,* his final attack upon the Bible. He claimed that the mind is made up of judgment, memory, and imagination. When we are asleep, judgment dozes, memory rouses occasionally, but imagination stays wide awake. His conclusion was, "It is absurd to place reliance upon dreams, and more so to make them the foundation of religion."

Actually, about thirty years earlier one of Paine's dreams was so vivid that he described it to a stranger. The man interpreted it for Paine, saying it showed the troubles the young nation was going to go through. Paine was impressed enough to record the whole story in his diary. The interpretation fit reality well enough, but it was too general to be highly convincing.

Paine suffered ruined health and a collapsed career after a year of nightmare imprisonment during the French Revolution, and therefore his "Essay on Dreams" was largely ignored. He claimed that critics did not dare to attack it because that would increase sales for him. *The Kingdom of Dreams* reports that in 1811 the essay was published in England; the publisher was sentenced to three years in jail and a six thousand dollar fine, and Paine remained in America.[1] That is an understatement; he had died in 1809.

Paine had requested burial in a Quaker cemetery because, in his words, the Episcopalians were too arrogant and the Presbyterians were too hypocritical. The local Quakers, perhaps afraid that their cemetery would be vandalized or scandalized if he were buried in it, suggested that it would be better for him to be buried elsewhere so that he could have a monument. Paine had to be buried alone on some unused land, and his bones were later moved and lost by an eccentric admirer. Before Paine died, he had fretted that his old bones would probably get lost, and he was right.

"Essay on Dreams" is almost as lost as Paine's bones; it is not included in most collections of his work. His editor Howard Fast explains that it is only of "antique" interest. Apparently this means that to republish Paine's attack on dreams in the Bible today would be beating a dead horse. Most people are no longer even acquainted with the dreams that Paine was denouncing.

Early Bible Dreams

In the creation story in Genesis 1, the earth seems at first to be vaguely and darkly asleep, and God calls it to form and life in a series of six days separated by evenings and mornings that we cannot imagine. On the seventh day he rested. Through the remainder of the Bible humans are acting and resting, acting and resting. And when humans rest, they dream. A few of these dreams are recorded, but none are recorded in the Bible's prehistory before Abraham.

The first and most important sleep the Bible mentions is the deep sleep of Adam when God created Eve from his side. Whether one takes this literally or figuratively, it is likely that Adam dreamed. Tertullian, the great defender of the faith around 200 A.D., taught in *A Treatise on the Soul* (in which eight chapters were about sleep and dreaming) that the Hebrew in Genesis 2:21 means that God sent a dream to Adam. Tertullian's books had a great influence upon the early church. Therefore it is likely that early Christians understood Adam's sleep as Tertullian did.[2] Later, when Adam and Eve chose to disobey God, they radically altered their states of consciousness. Whether one takes the Fall in the Garden literally or figuratively, it meant the fall of dreamers.

The next sleep described in the Bible was the drunken sleep that Noah fell into long after the flood. Noah's son Ham was cursed because, when he found Noah in a naked stupor, he called his brothers instead of covering the old man privately. Drunken sleep lacks healthy dreaming. Noah's drugged sleep was one of the few tragic sleep stories in the Bible.

Abraham is, of course, the first absolutely historical man in the Bible, and the first in the Bible to have a dream recorded. He lived perhaps four thousand years ago. God came to Abraham in a night vision and had him look at the stars, and God gave him a promise for his descendants. Because the Bible is very casual about distinguishing between waking visions and sleeping dreams, many people assume that Abraham was asleep and others assume that he was awake for this first great vision of God. We know that he was asleep for the next one. Abraham prepared and protected the animal sacrifices that God asked for, after the first vision, and fell into a deep sleep at sundown. In the darkness and dread God spoke clearly to Abraham, affirming the central promise of the Old Testament. This is the one account of God speaking to Abraham that seems definitely set in a dream state.

God spoke to Abraham in various rather direct ways. He used a sleeping dream to speak to one of Abraham's neighbors. God spoke to King Abimelech in a dream to warn him that his new concubine, Sarah, was really the wife of Abraham and that he must return her to her husband or he and his people would be destroyed. Abimelech promptly obeyed his dream.

It seems appropriate throughout the Bible that the Hebrew word for dream (*chalom,* or the verb *chalam*) is related to the Aramaic and Hebrew verb that means to be made healthy or strong. The first two sleeping dreams clearly cited in Genesis, Abraham's and Abimelech's, promised strong issue to one and saved the other from death.

The Lord appeared to Abraham's son Isaac at night (Genesis 26) to repeat the promise. Perhaps that was in a dream, perhaps not.

One of the most famous dreams in Scripture came to Isaac's son Jacob (Genesis 28) when he left his parents to join his Uncle Laban and slept on the way with his head on a stone and dreamed of a ladder to heaven. God spoke kindly to him in the dream, and Jacob named the place Bethel.

Laurens van der Post, reflecting on his boyhood, claimed, " . . . the dream of Jacob and the ladder to me was and remains the greatest of all dreams ever dreamt." He said he could easily have been talked and teased out of his childhood belief in the importance of dreams if it had not been for this dream in particular, and in general for the significant role allotted to dreams in the stories of the Old Testament he knew by heart and treasured long before he could be fed on easier fare such as the Brothers Grimm, Andrew Lang, and Hans Anderson.[3]

Twenty years after Jacob's ladder, God appeared to Jacob in a dream about sheep and reminded him of their dream encounter at Bethel, telling him it was time to leave his uncle and return to the land of his birth. Laban chased Jacob but did not use force on him because God had spoken to Laban in the night, in or out of a dream, and warned him to leave Jacob alone. Later, the night before Jacob was reunited with the brother he had cheated twenty years before, he wrestled all night with God and had his name changed to Israel. Perhaps he was wide awake; many people believe that this was a struggle in a dream.

Jacob's favorite son was Joseph, the prince of dreamers. As a boy Joseph dreamed twice in symbols about his large family honoring him, and his brothers resented it when he told them his dreams. Later, when Joseph was in prison in Egypt and two of his fellow prisoners were upset because they had dreams that needed interpretation, Joseph said, "Do not interpretations belong to God? Tell them to me, I pray you." Genesis 40:8, RSV. Both dreams foretold the future, and Joseph's interpretations proved correct three days later. The *Eerdmans Handbook to the Bible* includes a photograph of an Egyptian dream manual from the time of Joseph. It lists good and bad dreams in columns with their interpretations. Joseph, of course, did not use such books.

After two years had passed, Joseph was called upon to interpret a dream that bothered the Pharaoh. This also was a precognitive dream. Because of the wisdom of his interpretation, in which he attributed the dream and its interpretation to God, Joseph was elevated from prisoner to ruler of the land of Egypt. And when Joseph finally sent for his elderly father Jacob to come to live with him in the affluence of Egypt, God spoke to Jacob in visions of the night, probably dreams, encouraging him to make the move with his family.

So it was that the patriarchs dreamed their way from Ur to Egypt.

The next major figure in Old Testament history was Moses, who was called to lead the tribe back up out of Egypt four hundred years later, which may have been about 1300 B.C. God said to Moses and his sister and brother who helped him, "If there is a prophet among you, I the Lord make myself known to him in a vision, I speak with him in a dream. Not so with my servant Moses. . . . With him I speak mouth to mouth, clearly, and not in dark speech; and he beholds the form of the Lord" (Numbers 12:6–8, RSV). Needless to say, the Bible passages about Moses and his work lack the emphasis upon dreams that was found in Genesis.

Because of a strange error two of the books of Moses were used for centuries to discourage Christians from considering their dreams. In 375 A.D. Jerome, a lover of Roman literature, became very sick and dreamed that he appeared before the judgment seat of Christ. He was severely lashed because he preferred the writing of Cicero to the Bible. He promised to read only the Bible in the future and woke up black and blue from the bruises of the beating. Faithful to his promise, he became a great Bible scholar and produced the Latin Vulgate translation. Although he had rabbis helping him with the Old Testament, he inserted warnings against observing dreams in two places where such warnings did not belong.

Leviticus 19:26–27 says, "You must eat nothing with blood in it. You must not practice divination or magic. You are not to round off your hair at the edges nor trim the edges of your beard . . ." (Jerusalem Bible). In place of the warning against magic, Jerome substituted a warning about paying attention to dreams. He did the same thing in Deuteronomy 18:10.

In Deuteronomy 13:1–3,5 there is a valid warning about the misuse of dreams, in which the law of Moses states that if any prophet or dreamer tries to lead the people to worship foreign gods, that prophet or dreamer must be put to death for heresy. A similar warning against the misuse of dreams to lead people into heresy comes later in Jeremiah 23.

Joshua took over when Moses died and led the people into the promised land, in about 1250 B.C. God promosed Joshua, when he commissioned him for this task, "This book of the law shall not depart out of your mouth, but you shall meditate on it day and night, that you may be careful to do according to all that is written in it; for then you shall make your way prosperous, and then you shall have good success." Joshua 1:8, RSV. Is it possible that Joshua was to meditate upon the book in his sleep? Now, over three thousand years later, we have learned that the mind does "meditate" in various ways through the night.

The period of leadership by occasional judges followed the death of Joshua. Gideon, the sixth of these, was aided by a dream in rescuing Israel from the Midianites. The Midianites were a multitude and Gideon was leader of a tiny band, but God caused Gideon to go down at night and overhear one of the Midianites telling his comrade a dream he had, and the comrade interpreted the dream as a foretelling that Gideon would miraculously manage to conquer the multitude. With that assurance Gideon did it.

The last of the judges, the man who probably recorded their histories, was Samuel. When he was a boy, there was a dearth of words and visions from God. One night he kept thinking that his foster-father the priest was calling for him, but it was God who called, "Samuel! Samuel!" every time he went back to bed. It is a fact that some people hear their names called as they begin to drift into dreams, in hypnagogic imagery. What Samuel heard from God, a valid prophetic message, could certainly have come in that way.

Dreams of the Kingdom and Dreams in Captivity

All his adult life, Samuel was noted for being a seer, and God revealed to him who would be the first king of Israel. We aren't told if Samuel's messages from God all came at night, but the message about how King Saul had displeased God certainly did. That may well have been in a dream.

Saul was mentally ill and finally killed himself shortly before

1000 B.C. His successor David wrote "I bless the Lord who gives me counsel; in the night also my heart instructs me" (Psalm 16:7, RSV). We can only conjecture about what David meant.

One night David's advisor Nathan had a night vision, in which God revealed that David should not build a temple. That was probably a message in a dream. David obeyed.

David's son Solomon took the throne in 961 B.C. Then God appeared to Solomon in a dream and asked him what gift he would choose. Solomon chose a wise and discerning mind, and God granted the request, adding a promise of riches and honor as well. When Solomon awoke, he knew it had been a dream, but it was true.

The title of Psalm 127 indicates that it was written by Solomon. The Jerusalem Bible translates it this way:

In vain you get up earlier,
and put off going to bed,
sweating to make a living,
since he provides for his beloved as they sleep.

This is an excellent translation, and it is a fitting statement from Solomon, who knowingly received great blessing from God in his dream.

Years later, when Solomon had finished building the temple, God appeared to him again in the same way, warning him in greater detail that he must live in integrity or ruin would come. Because Solomon ignored the dream warning and dabbled in idolatry, "the Lord was angry with Solomon, because his heart had turned away from the Lord, the God of Israel, who had appeared to him twice" (I Kings 11:9, RSV). Most people who read that statement probably don't consider that those two appearances in the past that were so important in God's judgment were both in Solomon's sleeping dreams.

The pessimistic book of Ecclesiastes, by the way, scoffs at dreams. We cannot be sure that this book is by Solomon, as was traditionally believed. It would be strange for Solomon, of all people, to take dreams lightly.

The Song of Solomon, often called The Song of Songs, is another book that may have been written by Solomon. Those who are touched by Solomon's words in Psalm 127, "he provides for his beloved as they sleep," may hear a response in the words of the bride:

I sleep, but my heart is awake.
I hear my Beloved knocking.
    The Song of Solomon 5:2, Jerusalem Bible

Christians usually take this as the response of the church to Christ.

After Solomon's tragic lapses and his death in 925 B.C. the kingdom split and went into decline. Prophets tried to minister to the two kingdoms. The prophet Eiijah became so discouraged that he gave up at one point in his dramatic ministry; then an angel twice touched him in his sleep, offering him potent nourishment that enabled him to walk for forty days to Sinai. When Elijah retired for the night in a cave on Sinai, God came to him and gave him the motivation and instructions for going on as the prophet to Israel. We don't know if Elijah was dreaming that night in the cave. Many people assume God came there in dreams.

Over a century after Elijah Israel fell to Assyria. Finally Judah fell to Babylon. It was the surrender of Judah to Babylon in 597 B.C. that began the story of Daniel, the most dream-centered book in the Bible. Daniel and some other outstanding young men from Judah were carried off to the palace of King Nebuchadnezzar of Babylon for three years of education in the Babylonian language so they could become government servants. God had given Daniel the gift of understanding visions and dreams.

In the familiar old story King Nebuchadnezzar was greatly troubled by a dream he could not recall and ordered all his advisors to be executed because no one could reveal his forgotten dream to him. Daniel and his friends were included in the decree, although they had not been consulted. God gave Daniel the answer in a vision in the night, which itself may have been a dream. Daniel then went to the king and explained that God had revealed the future to the king in his forgotten dream. Daniel described a giant statue to the king and told him that his rule was the golden head, which would be followed by other empires of less value. This so pleased the king that he made Daniel his chief advisor.

Later Nebuchadnezzar had a nightmare about a great tree and a terrible message from an angel. He told the dream to Daniel, who

perceived its meaning right away. Daniel warned the king that he
was the tree, which was in danger. If the king did not stop sinning
and start to help the poor, he would have to live in the wilderness
like an animal for seven years. Apparently the king dismissed the
matter. One year later he was struck with severe mental illness for
seven years, as Daniel had predicted. At the end of the seven
years, as predicted, he regained his sanity and turned to the God
of Daniel as his authority.

There is a strange account in modern dream annals about a
scholar of ancient Assyrian, Dr. Hilprecht, to whom a Babylonian
priest appeared one night in a dream. Among other things the
priest allegedly told Hilprecht that the modern understanding of
the name Nebuchadnezzar was wrong. Scholars thought it had to
do with masonry, but in fact it meant "Nebo, protect my bound-
aries."

The year when Nebuchadnezzar died and his son Belshazzar
became king, Daniel had a dream at night that he wrote down and
kept secret. It was about four beasts representing future empires,
and it left Daniel pale. Two years later Daniel had a similar experience, probably another dream, about a goat attacking a ram, and
the angel Gabriel explained to Daniel the future world events this
symbolized. Daniel was so overwhelmed that he remained sick in
bed for several days afterward.

The rest of Daniel's adventures don't specifically mention
sleeping dreams. We aren't told whether he or the lions dreamed
any the night they spent in a pit together, but we are told that
King Darius (who wanted Daniel to serve as his prime minister)
didn't sleep a wink until he was sure of Daniel's safety the next
morning.

In *The Age of Reason* Thomas Paine pointed out both Daniel
and Ezekiel as prisoners-of-war in a foreign country. Their purported dreams, he reasoned, were a kind of code they resorted to
in order to communicate political projects and opinions and information safely. "They pretended to have dreamed dreams and seen
visions, because it was unsafe for them to speak facts or plain
language."

Two other books of the Old Testament that may have been
written around 500 B.C. are Esther and Job.

The book of Esther, as it appears in the Protestant Bibles, mentions neither God nor dreams. However, the Roman Catholic versions of Esther include an introduction and conclusion from an early Greek text that frame the story in a prophetic dream God gave to Esther's uncle Mordecai before the story began. The symbolic dream came true in the course of Esther's adventures, under Mordecai's wise guidance in response to God's leading.

Although the swashbuckling story of Esther and Mordecai and Xerxes (also called Ahasuerus) is often suspected of being fictitious, Xerxes himself figures in the history of his day. According to the historian Herodotus, after inheriting the Persian throne Xerxes was haunted by a dream that commanded him to go to war against Greece. His uncle Artabanus advised him that the dreams were no divine command but only his own daytime ideas breaking through at night. Xerxes convinced his uncle to wear the king's clothes and sleep in his bed and see if the dream came to him also. Artabanus's dream accused him of false concern for his nephew's welfare and warned him to let the foolish king do what he pleased, threatening his eyes with red hot pokers. The uncle ran to his nephew and urged him to go ahead with his plans. In this Artabanus was purposely abandoning his nephew to trouble.

Xerxes taxed his people and prepared for four years, purportedly starting out for the invasion with almost two million men. They pillaged Athens, but they were defeated at Salamis in 480 B.C. This was the beginning of the end of the great Persian empire. Xerxes reigned another fifteen years before he was killed, and it was during that time that Esther became his queen.

The book of Job cannot be definitely set anywhere in history, but it is revered as a deeply profound story from the distant past. In it Job complains to God about bad dreams on top of all his waking misery.

When I say, "My bed will comfort me,
my couch will ease my complaint,"
then thou dost scare me with dreams
and terrify me with visions...."
    Job 7:13–14, RSV

Many people quote the words of Elihu, later in the book, to

illustrate the Bible's strong endorsement of dreams as messages
from God. Lovely as the passage is, there is serious disagreement
about the correctness and appropriateness of Elihu's sermon to
Job. God cuts into Elihu's speech after it has gone on long enough,
and it is never mentioned again. Elihu's point about dreams is that
God speaks to us in two ways that are not direct: through our
dreams and through our suffering.

Why do you contend against him,
    saying, "He will answer none of my words"?
For God speaks in one way,
    and in two, though man does not perceive it.
In a dream, in a vision of the night,
    when deep sleep falls upon men,
    while they slumber on their beds,
then he opens the ears of men,
    and terrifies them with warnings,
that he may turn man aside from his deed,
    and cut off pride from man;
he keeps back his soul from the Pit,
    his life from perishing by the sword.
      Job 33:13–18, RSV

Significantly, in this passage a "vision of the night" is clearly
identified as sleeping dreams. That emphasizes the likelihood that
visions of the night usually refers to sleeping dreams in the Old
Testament. No one knows how many of the visions of the prophets came in dreams. The Hebrew language and thought pattern do
not tell us.

Dreams of the New Testament

About five hundred years after the angel Gabriel visited Daniel
in Babylon, Gabriel visited Zechariah the priest to foretell the
birth of John the Baptist and later appeared to Mary to foretell the
birth of Jesus. Next, an angel (we are not told if it was Gabriel)
appeared to Joseph in a sleeping dream and instructed him to
marry Mary, although she was pregnant. Joseph did not hesitate
to obey his dream.

After the wise men from the East came to worship the child

Jesus, they were warned in a dream to flee the country instead of revealing to King Herod where the holy child was. They obeyed.

Next an angel came to Joseph in a dream for the second time and warned him to flee to Egypt to escape Herod, which he did immediately. After Herod's death in 4 B.C. an angel appeared to Joseph in a dream the third time and told him to return to his homeland, which he did. But in a fourth dream he was warned that Judea would be too dangerous, and so he settled his family in Nazareth of Galilee instead. Four times the earthly father of Jesus obeyed God's messages in dreams.

At the end of Jesus' life the wife of Pilate, the Roman official who oversaw Judea, urged her husband to avoid taking any part in his persecution. She had suffered greatly in a dream about Jesus and knew he was innocent. Nevertheless, Pilate gave in to the will of the mob.

The next mention of dreams occurs in Acts 2. Jesus had died and been resurrected and after forty days had been lifted up. The disciples were waiting in Jerusalem, and on Pentecost they were filled with the Holy Spirit. Peter preached his famous sermon winning three thousand people to Christ. He began that sermon with a quotation from the prophet Joel that was possibly five hundred years old then:

And in the last days it shall be, God declares,
that I will pour out my Spirit upon all flesh,
and your sons and your daughters shall prophesy,
and your young men shall see visions,
and your old men shall dream dreams,
yea on my menservants and my maidservants in those days
I will pour out my Spirit; and they shall prophesy. . . .
    Acts 2:17–18, RSV

Peter told the crowd that this prophecy was finally fulfilled.

Peter himself soon became the subject of a most memorable *non*dream story. Once, before Herod Antipus died in 39 A.D., he imprisoned Peter, intending to kill him as he had killed James, brother of John. There were four squads of soldiers guarding Peter where he lay asleep in his cell chained to two soldiers. An angel lit up the cell and hit Peter to awaken him. The chains fell off.

Peter obeyed every order from the angel, assuming it was all a dream. He thought that he was having one of those interesting experiences of lucid dreaming in which the dreamer knows that he is only dreaming. They passed all the guards, and the iron gate opened for them automatically.

Only when the angel left him alone in the street did Peter realize that he wasn't dreaming after all. It had been a miracle. In the morning the soldiers were mystified, and Herod ordered that they would have to die for letting Peter get away. Acts does not tell us if any of them escaped.

There are dozens of visions recorded in the Bible which could have taken place in sleeping dreams, and one of the most important is recorded in Acts 16. Paul was on his second missionary journey, probably with Silas, Luke, and Timothy, when a man of Macedonia appeared to him in a vision at night begging him to come across the Aegean Sea to Greece. Paul and his friends took this as a message from God and started on the trip as soon as possible. This led, among other things, to the founding of the churches at Phillipi, Thessalonica, and Corinth, where Paul formed his close friendship with Priscilla and Aquilla. It was in Corinth that God told Paul in another night vision, "Do not be afraid, but speak and do not be silent; for I am with you, and no man shall attack you to harm you; for I have many people in this city" (Acts 18:9, RSV). So Paul taught there for a year and a half.

Getting at Truth

When Paul finally left Corinth, he went next to Ephesus. Later he wrote his letter to the Ephesians. The section of that letter that we know today as the fifth chapter, which includes Paul's admonitions about mutual submission among Christians and proper marital relationships, has received a great deal of attention from both Christians who believe in female subordination to males and those who do not. Equally sincere Christians find support for very different points of view in this passage.

Elisabeth Elliot is a leading exponent of the doctrine that roles should be determined by gender and that domesticity and submission are the only proper way of life for women in the home and the church. I believe in role flexibility for men and women depending upon talents and needs, a view set forth in my book *Up from Eden* and in Christian author Letha Scanzoni's *All We're Meant To Be*.

At the beginning of February 1976 Letha Scanzoni dreamed about her old friend Elisabeth Elliot. The very next night she dreamed that I was going about with a revolutionary new insight into Paul's teaching in Ephesians 5. The passage says in verse 23, "the husband is the head of the wife as Christ is the head of the church," and in verse 27, "that he might present the church to himself in splendor, *without spot or wrinkle*. [emphasis added]. . . ." (RSV). In Scanzoni's dream I was announcing to anyone who would listen that that passage proves that husbands should wash and iron the clothes for their wives. Christian men are all supposed to do the laundry if they believe in Paul's view of marriage in Ephesians 5.

Scanzoni's ingenious and outlandish interpretation of Scripture is probably quite a rare kind of dream, and I take it to be a good-natured satire upon the way some people really mishandle Scripture in their waking lives. It seems that Scanzoni turned the tables on some of her critics in the privacy of her dream, recruiting me to do the job for her. Whatever else the dream meant, it is an excellent case of imaginative wit made possible by intimate knowledge of the Bible. But it raises the question of how often we think about Bible passages in our dreams. That is a serious question touched on in Chapter 10.

What struck me as most peculiar about Scanzoni's dream was that, on January 29, 1976, Professor J. R. Christopher had written me a letter concerning C. S. Lewis, in which he quoted the Bible in a poetic way and then signed off by promising to enjoy grading freshman themes if I would enjoy washing clothes. I sent him some sassy reply immediately, challenging him to learn to wash clothes, as I know how to grade freshman themes. On February 3 he wrote again, claiming that his wife wouldn't let him near her new washer because of a couple of mistakes he made with her old one. It was during this playful exchange of letters between California and Texas that Scanzoni had her related dream in Indiana. When Scanzoni's letter arrived telling me about her dream, I was highly amused and also considered it a mysterious coincidence.

The last book in the Bible is the one that has provoked the most bewildering array of commentaries. John's Revelation came to him either in a mystical vision or a sleeping dream or some other state that we do not know about. In his discussion of the need for fantasy and mystery in our lives in his book *Orthodoxy,* G. K. Chesterton said, with slight exaggeration perhaps, "There is a notion adrift that imagination, especially mystical imagination, is dangerous to man's mental balance.... Imagination does not breed insanity.... Everywhere we see that men do not go mad by dreaming.... And though St. John the Evangelist saw many strange monsters in his vision, he saw no creature so wild as one of his own commentators."[4]

Commentators have been interpreting Scripture both tamely and wildly in the Christian Church since its very early years. One of the most tumultuous times for this was the fourth century when the heresy (or truth) of Arianism threatened (or promised) to take over. Arius taught that Jesus was once created by God and was a being more than an ordinary man but less than God. Although his view was defeated in 325 A.D. at the Council of Nicea, it refused to remain defeated and became the official theology briefly at the middle of the century. That made it wrong to believe in the Trinity!

Three church leaders who were lifelong friends, from what is now eastern Turkey, played the main role in finally defeating Arianism and permanently establishing the doctrine of the Trinity; they were Basil, his brother Gregory of Nyssa, and his friend Gregory of Nazianzen. These men owed a lot to dreams. Gregory of Nazianzen wrote once about his early life, "And God summoned me from boyhood in my nocturnal dreams, and I arrived at the very goals of wisdom." Gregory of Nyssa claimed that dreams usually conform to the state of one's character; they are not formed by the intellect, "but by the less rational disposition of the soul." Basil likened dream interpretation to understanding difficult scriptures.[5]

Valens, the Emperor of the East, and his wife Dominicica were Arians and enemies of Basil's theology. They persecuted him. Then, if the story is true, Dominicica had a dream in which God threatened to take away her only son if they continued to mistreat Basil. This warning saved Basil from further danger at their hands.

Basil's own words about dreams and the meaning of Scripture were these: "The enigmas in dreams have a close affinity to those things which are signified in an allegoric or hidden sense in the Scriptures. Thus both Joseph and Daniel, through the gift of prophecy, used to interpret dreams, since the force of reason by itself is not powerful enough for getting at truth."[6]

"The force of reason by itself is not powerful enough for getting at truth." That is what Thomas Paine lacked the intuition to believe. Reason is a great good, but it is not enough.

Notes

1. Josephine and Philippa Duke Schuyler, *The Kingdom of Dreams* (New York: Award Books, 1968), p. 105.

2. Morton Kelsey, *op, cit..*, pp. 241–248.

3. Laurens van der Post, *op. cit.,* pp. 12–13.

4. G. K. Chesterton, *Orthodoxy* (Garden City, New York: Doubleday Anchor, 1959), pp. 16–17.

5. Morton Kelsey discusses the attitude of these three men and a fourth, Chrysostom, in *Dreams: the Dark Speech of the Spirit* (Garden City, New York: Doubleday, 1968), pp. 132–139. A passage by Gregory of Nyssa is provided by Kelsey in the appendix, pp. 252–257. This book is now published as *God, Dreams and Revelation* (Minneapolis: Augsburg, 1974).

6. Kelsey, *op. cit.,* p. 136.

FIVE

LEARNING THE LANGUAGE: FOREIGN IDEAS

Somehow it seems to fill my head with ideas—only I don't exactly know what they are!

Lewis Carroll, *Alice's Adventures in Wonderland*

Knowledge and Trust

Late in 1975 I had a dream in a foreign language. There wasn't a word of English in it. I couldn't tell what language it was much less what people were saying. In my sleep I felt it was very funny to dream in a language I didn't know. After awakening, I felt the whole thing had been rather a cheat. Obviously a dream can't tell me anything if it doesn't speak my language. It seemed worthless.

Much later a meaning of that dream occurred to me. The dream was a teasing reminder that no dream can tell me its meaning unless I know enough of its language. This was a hint to pay more attention to learning the language of dreams.

Most of us live most of our waking lives in prose, but we dream more in poetry. Poetry tends to be intense, complex, many layered, and symbolic. Even dull dreams come to us in poetic language. (That does not mean that they are necessarily sublime, or even dignified.)

C. S. Lewis wrote about the difference between ordinary language, scientific language, and poetic language: "Such information as Poetic language has to give can be received only if you are ready to meet it half way," Lewis warned. "It is no good holding a dialectical pistol to the poet's head and demanding how the deuce a river could have hair, or thought be green, or a woman a red rose. ... If he had anything to tell you, you will never get it by behaving that way. You must begin by trusting him."[1]

In one of my dreams in 1978 I stated that to understand dream content one must trust dreams. My husband speculated to me that taking time to work with memories of dreams is equivalent to taking time to read, because they are similarly educational. I answered, "Yes, and the *space* we give to consciously remembered dreams is very efficiently used." As I said that, I was seeing the extremely compact storage of large colored posters, which are, I was aware, "diagrams of reality." (I had no suspicion that I was a figure in a "poster" myself; I thought I was awake.) I concluded the dream by remarking that it would be a great waste of time to try to work anything out with Mary Jane Mann, because those posters are not useful to anyone who is not sympathetic to them. Clearly, one has to be sympathetic to dreams, which are like posters, to see them as "diagrams of reality."

My husband's opening remark about time was probably referring to the fact that in real life he has recently succeeded in increasing our sons' reading time, and we have recently succeeded in increasing our own dream work time. In my response about poster storage space, I was probably referring to the incredibly tiny submicroscopic space that every dream memory takes up in our brains.

What was Mann doing in there, aside from the fact that she had been mentioned to me just before my dream? (She once brought C. S. Lewis's friend Sister Penelope all the way from England to California to see the Rose Parade from a grandstand seat of honor, only to have Sister Penelope decide after her arrival that she didn't care to go to the parade.) First, I asked what *Mann* means to me and realized that it usually means the author Thomas Mann. Thomas Mann used to refer to waking thought as daylight grammar and to dreams as moon grammar. To me *Thomas* means doubter, and so I associate Mann with doubting. Second, Mary Jane means rationalism to me, as explained in Chapter Eight. Third, Mary Jane Mann directs the local Y; she represents it and promotes it. In my dreams the letter *Y* sometimes stands for "Why?" So it is futile to try to get unsympathetic doubters who care most about "Why?" to work on understanding dreams.

Needless to say, I don't believe everything I hear myself say in dreams, even about dreams. C. S. Lewis once said that a cabbage, being a product of botany, is not therefore qualified to give a lecture on botany. However, I think a botanist's dream of a cabbage's lecture on botany might be well worth listening to and considering.

Language and Symbols

It is obvious that what one discusses or experiences in dreams is apt to be material one has dealt with in waking life. When it is not so, we note those exceptions. The blind and deaf Helen Keller said that often in her dreams distant and silent thoughts would pass through her mind like shadows. She wondered if they were ghosts of thoughts some ancestor had thought.

"The more I learned, the oftener I dreamed," she said. She said she sometimes suffered from quizzes in her dreams, and she recorded one of the difficult questions: "What was the name of the first mouse that worried Hippopotamus, satrap of Cambridge under Astyagas, grandfather of Cyrus the Great?" She said she awoke in terror because she couldn't answer.[2]

Sometimes, Helen Keller said, the things she had learned and the things she had been taught dropped away in her dreams like a lizard's old skin, and she saw her soul as God sees it.

Another blind and deaf woman, Laura Bridgman of the Perkins Institute for the Blind, learned the hand and finger language designed for such people. She was observed to use it with great rapidity when she was asleep. This was her way of talking in her sleep, surely bedroom sleep.

These women have had to learn about reality with very limited symbols. Unfortunately, they were gone before dream researchers could probe the nature of their dream imagery.

Perhaps no one has a collection of dreams by blind and deaf dreamers, but if anyone did it would be Calvin Hall of the Institute of Dream Research in Santa Cruz. He is one of the major authorities on dreams in the United States today. He has collected, classified, ranked, and interpreted tens of thousands of dreams, separated into groups by the dreamers' sex, race, profession, and many other characteristics.

Hall claims that most dreams are ordinary realistic situations in which people are talking coherently about their activities. I was amazed by his claim that people don't often work, shop for food and clothing, visit public buildings, or include famous people in their dreams. I do those things very frequently in my dreams, and so do people I know. There is an entire book made up of dreams that British people have had about the current royal family. I recently had a dream about Calvin Hall himself telling me where he went to college. (I seriously suspect that my glorious pageant of Swiss theology and psychology took place in an auditorium called Calvin Hall, although I am not quite positive. This pun is typical of plays on names in dreams.)

Hall's view of the meaning of dreams is intimately connected with his view of the meaning of life. Hall is basically Freudian, although he rejects Freud's belief that dreams are trying to hide their meanings. The dream state merely reveals more clearly the wishes and fears that guide our actions in real life, Hall claimed in his 1953 book *The Meaning of Dreams*.

In his essay "Out of a Dream Came the Faucet" Hall discusses a young man's dream in which a water faucet was a symbol for a penis. He says that such a symbol is too obvious to be a disguise. Every faucet in dreams or real life represents a penis, according to Hall. Faucets were not invented to be a convenient source of water.

Everyone knows the truism, "Necessity is the mother of invention." Hall seems to believe that infantile wishes (often about mother) are the mother of invention. The inventor of real faucets, Hall explains, was purposely creating a kind of fantasy toy penis that could be turned on and off at will. It is an accident of history, Hall believes, that this penis symbol turned out to have a practical use after it was invented. Likewise, Hall believes, money was invented by someone who wanted to collect lots of feces. Rockets to the moon were invented by men who wanted to have sex with their mothers. Houses were invented by people who really wanted to return to the womb. It was a pleasant bonus for the first house builders, apparently, when they found out that houses could protect them from the weather and serve as shelters.[3]

To some of us Hall's use of symbols in explaining human history seems as arbitrary as Humpty Dumpty's abuse of language in *Alice's Adventures in Wonderland:*

"There's glory for you!"

"I don't know what you mean by 'glory.'" Alice said.

Humpty Dumpty smiled contemptuously. "Of course you don't—till I tell you. I meant 'there's a nice knock-down argument.'"

"But 'glory' doesn't mean 'a nice knock-down argument,'" Alice objected.

"When *I* use a word," Humpty Dumpty said, in a rather scornful tone, "it means just what I choose it to mean—neither more nor less."

"The question is," said Alice, "whether you *can* make words mean so many different things."

"The question is," said Humpty Dumpty, "which is to be master—that's all."

In our dreams, if not in waking life, some of us act just like Humpty Dumpty with words, and at those times we need to respect the Humpty Dumpty meanings and make a note of them. Novel uses of words are neologisms.

In a recent dream I heard William James, the great American psychologist, saying, "If she does not talk too much, a woman is an abject companion on a honeymoon." I heard what James meant as well as what he said, and what he meant was "If she does not talk too much, a woman is a useful companion on a honeymoon." The word *abject* was either a Humpty Dumpty or a freudian slip. James meant that a woman is useful on a honeymoon if you have children to tend to. The day before I dreamed this I learned that

James used his own honeymoon for starting to write his first book. In my dreams books in process appear as babies and children, and so it is no wonder that I had James taking a child on his honeymoon and wanting his bride to keep quiet.

One night I dreamed that I ate a tasty little "cheese replica," something like a small taco. Much later I recalled that, as an art lover, I have sometimes referred to a shoddy reproduction of a great work of art as a cheesy replica. I rather suspect that I gave my dream snack that name because it was not genuine food—through no fault of its own.

Another arbitrary use of words that can appear in dreams is the literal definition of a term used inappropriately and then built on. In one dream I was at the home of some cat owners, admiring their various cats. Finally the most beautiful cat I have ever seen walked across the living room, just as alive and catlike as all the others from the same litter. But this one had layers and layers of bits of gorgeous colored cloth all over instead of fur. It was fascinating. Being interested in genetics, I told the owners very seriously that it was obvious that this cat's mother had mated with a patchwork quilt. I thought it was a splendid example of eugenics. After I awakened I realized that my glorious genetic engineering idea was just a particularly beautiful manifestation of the term *calico cat.*

Correspondences

I have a theory that the reason many of our dreams lose their coherency when we awaken is that they depend upon subtle correlations, many of which we cannot maintain or even recreate while awake. They are often too original for us. We dismiss them as incongruous when really they are extremely congruous in unexpected ways.

Charles Darwin's cousin, Sir Francis Galton (1822–1911), whose IQ is estimated to have been 200, used to amuse himself by replacing numerals with distinct smells and then doing math with odors instead of numerals. For example, if he replaced *one* with the smell of peppermint, *two* with the scent of roses, and *three* with the odor of new-mown hay, then peppermint plus roses equals new-mown hay. He would not even have to think of the words for the smells. Galton managed to block out numerals completely when amusing himself this way. Of course he went on into fairly complex problems in his game. Eventually he published a paper on this trick called "Arithmetic by Smell."[4] Without a good explanation any quotation from this unique but accurate kind of math would sound like insane nonsense. If a child had asked Galton, "How much is four and five?" Galton could have absent-mindedly answered something like "mothballs." Galton was that sophisticated, and so are some of our dreams.

When I learned about Galton, I felt better about a dream I had once concerning the home and its occupants that had been the second residence to the left of my home in San Diego when I was a child, and the home and its occupants that had been the second residence to the right of my home in Santa Ana when I was a child. In my dream the two cities and two times seemed like one. The dream concerned the serious health problems of a little girl in the first example and an elderly lady in the second, all historically accurate and seemingly rational. The only odd thing about this dream, aside from combining two locales and times into one, was that, as it ended, I knew that all the elements in it corresponded perfectly to certain organs in my body, according to their location and their condition at specific times in my life. Unfortunately, I could not retain the vaguest idea, in my higher consciousness, about what the body information had been. Of course there is no way to know if the complicated analysis was accurate or fictitious.

Upon reflection it occurred to me that San Diego (Spanish for St. James) represents works to me (including intellectual work) because of the book of James in the New Testament. San Diego is where I learned to read and write and do mathematics. Santa Ana (St. Ann) represents the inner, little known part of the self to me, because Ann is my middle name. Furthermore, my home in Santa Ana previously belonged to my grandmother named Anna, who was to me a loving and mysterious person I rarely saw before she died. She was somewhat crippled.

It seems possible that one of the things this short but complex dream represented was facts about the left hemisphere of my brain, represented by San Diego, and the right hemisphere, represented by Santa Ana. I sustained mild physical damage in both brain hemispheres when I was in or near the corresponding neighborhoods of the dream. The trauma to my left hemisphere in San Diego damaged by ability to memorize words and numbers, and the trauma to my right hemisphere near Santa Ana weakened my left side. For all I know, the dream with its details about the two neighbors and their homes and illnesses was "a diagram of reality," describing the exact nature and specific location of the subtle brain damage. If that was not the meaning of the dream, something equally esoteric was. I knew that entire meaning one brief moment, then lost it forever. To me the idea that one can have a glimpse of such correlations is really more interesting than whatever information was in that glimpse.

A later dream illustrated such correspondences much more clearly, because it was very simple and I remembered it. I was walking along the sidewalk in silver shoes (representing fantasy to me) and asked a wise old woman to be my guide. She took me with her to a healer upstairs and gave me a notebook to use for communication. When the nurse asked me for my name, I was going to spell it on my notebook for her, but I saw that the notebook was a picture of bright scenery that needed to have figures of people added in the foreground. The only way to communicate with the nurse was to draw pictures of the members of a family into the colored scene to represent my name. When she asked me what each person represented, one by one, I could tell her the letters of my name. (This seems strikingly similar to the way a dream explains its images when we ask the right questions.) After we had done that, she told me that I must have left out one of the letters in my first name. I saw that she was right and said, "Yes, draw in a little boy, by all means, and name him Y!" I felt terrible that I had left out a member of my name.

This dream was obviously demonstrating for me how our dreams try to communicate with us in pictures. The pictures often spell out messages, but they are not necessarily perfect messages. It is obvious that the reason Y was represented as a little boy is that I heard "Why?" so often from my sons when they were little. I think the reason I left out that letter is that the question "Why?" rarely if ever occurs in my dreams. It runs counter to the dream experience. As soon as the nurse added the little boy named Y, my dream dissolved. That makes me suspect that, figuratively speaking, my dream self is *Kathrn* (rather than *Kathryn*) Lindskoog. The inquiring spirit that is an important part of me is rarely included.

It was the claim of P. D. Ouspensky, author of *A New Model of the Universe,* that one cannot ever say one's own name in a dream. In my opinion, almost all generalizations like that are false, and I suspect that it can be done. However, to my chagrin, I failed to give my name in a C. S. Lewis Society meeting that I attended in a dream in the summer of 1978. As those attending the meeting all introduced themselves in turn in the large circle, my turn came and I said, "I am C. S. Lewis and I am sorry I can't be here because I am dead." There were expressions of sincere regret from people who did not know yet that he had died in 1963. I was not deluded about my identity; it had simply been my duty to speak for Lewis.

Later in that meeting a young man said, "I know who you are. You're the author of the book with a lion on the cover." (That is correct.) In response a very dignified woman of my acquaintance burst out, "Honey, she was into this Lewis game before you were *born!*" It was a peculiar meeting indeed, partly because it turned out that this dream was written (I was living it not reading it) on "fold-a-note" stationery, which was creased. I think the outburst of the dignified woman occurred on a crease. The bottom third of the letter did not lie flat, but was bent upward at an angle of about forty-five degrees from the rest of the letter. Therefore, when I made a statement at the end, the people all broke into wild applause, and the sober meeting ended in merriment and levity because it was sticking up in the air.

Those who have claimed that dreams are letters to ourselves probably never thought about the angle of the letter in space determining its contents. That is the kind of strange dream correspondence and correspondences that boggles our waking minds. During the entire C. S. Lewis meeting, which took place in England as well as Los Angeles, and included C. S. Lewis's brother part of the time (he had been dead five years) and some of his handwriting at other times, I never wondered "Why?" about anything.

Night Traveling

The question "Why?" resides in the left hemisphere of the brain, which is the logical, mathematical, verbal half. The right half of the brain is spatial and intuitive, dealing with pictures and places. Tests have shown that during sleep the connector between the two halves of the brain, called the *corpus callosum,* becomes extraordinarily inactive. Usually it serves as an incredible trunkline of messages, coordinating the work of the two halves. In sleep the two halves are barely in touch with each other. This adds significance to the fact that "split-brain" people, who have had their corpus callosum severed for crucial medical reasons, claim that they never dream again. These people are stating that fact with their left halves, which control verbal expression. Dreaming certainly seems to be primarily a right-hemisphere experience. The left hemisphere stops dominating our thoughts at night.

One night I dreamed that I was driving on a dark six-lane divided highway for hours on end, and I was very tired. I remember vividly that I moved from the center lane to the right lane to let a fast truck go by in the center lane. Then I found a slow car in front of me and moved back to center. I increased speed, passed the car, and moved back to the right. In waking life I make such moves while thinking about other things, but in dream life I am absorbed in movements. (In dreams we seem to have one-track minds.) Then I hoped I would not have to drive too much longer. I thought, "I know what time it is. I know how fast I am going. But I do not have any idea how far it is from here to my home, so I cannot figure out what time I will get home." (This, of course, can easily be taken as a commentary upon where I am in life in relation to the final "going home," and I don't doubt that implication.) But then I thought, "It's just as well I don't know how far it is, because I would *not* do the math problem anyway." That was the conclusion of the dream.

I think the dream was a witty one. There was a very good reason for my refusing to calculate when I would get home, even if I had the data. The more I think about it, the more sure I am that the mathematical functions of my left hemisphere are simply not available to my predominately right-hemisphere dream consciousness. I feel positive that I have never solved a math problem of any kind in a dream. Apparently the verbal center in my left hemisphere is somewhat available much of the time, because the right hemisphere itself knows very few words and yet many of my dreams are full of words. They must come in from the left hemisphere.

A dream I had recently seemed to be commenting upon that very idea. In it, an extremely nice, intelligent Japanese boy came down on the sand in San Diego to join my nephews and me by the water's edge. I thought that he had just arrived in the United States but that he had studied English before moving here from Israel. He was carrying a large new art book that his mother had just bought him. It was full of color reproductions of the work of a great painter. To my surprise his mother had bought him the edition with printing all in Japanese instead of English. I planned to show the pictures to my nephews and explain them; luckily, I didn't have to depend upon captions for my understanding of art. My nephews told me that our friend had just left Japan three days ago. He spent two days in Israel. Then on the flight from Israel to the United States he had his only English lesson and learned two or three words. He did not fully realize how little English he knew. I understood why his new book was the Japanese rather than the English edition.

The right hemisphere is indeed like the newly arrived Japanese boy with a book of beautiful pictures that he is eager to share. He is a gracious and graceful person, but he does have what many of us consider an "inscrutable" way of thinking. He has less mastery of English than he realizes and he knows a difficult system of symbols that are unknown to us. We can learn from his pictures and enjoy his friendship. He is a foreigner to our way of thinking, but he obviously knows us already and likes us. If he is like some other Japanese people I have known of, he will sometimes concoct highly amusing phrases in his attempts to communicate in English. He comes to us by way of the Holy Land.

The right hemisphere seems to be a world traveler at night. Both Robert Louis Stevenson and Thomas DeQuincey have given us elaborate descriptions of the breathtaking travels that they took in their dreams. I think that I travel almost every night, although

I can't be sure, because I have very limited recall. I know I can range in one dream from the seashore to icy mountains. Sometimes I cross Europe, go up the West Coast, head south across Mexico (looking for Rio de Janeiro before I get to Tijuana), see strange sunsets in Switzerland, or, when I take my favorite trip, visit England again. I use all kinds of transportation and sometimes maps, restaurants, and luggage. I must visit hotels at least once a week! The last time I was in Chicago my city bus kept turning into a ship, which was appropriate because it had a deck on top replete with captain and life boats. Chicago has never been one of my best dreams, but some of the other places I visit seem like paradise. There is a depth, a clarity of color, a cast of light, a spiritual intensity that is refreshment to the soul.

My own night travels remind me in a mild way of De Quincey's reference to "nightly spectacles of more than earthly splendour" and "sometimes I seemed to have lived for seventy or a hundred years in one night."[5] Charles Lamb wrote, "My dreams . . . are of architecture and of buildings—cities abroad, which I have never seen, and hardly have hoped to see. I have traversed, for the seeming length of a natural day, Rome, Amsterdam, Paris, Lisbon —their churches, palaces, marketplaces, shops, suburbs, ruins, with an inexpressible sense of delight—a maplike distinctness of trace—and a daylight vividness of vision that was all but being awake."[6]

My friend Kathy Crosby, an extraordinary dreamer who has never been to Europe or taken any special interest in it, sent one of her daughters there for a three-month college tour. She soon found herself dreaming extremely frequently that she was in Europe observing Karen. She watched her in all kinds of activities in various countries—touring museums, walking in old streets, having fun in hotels with her friends. When Karen came home and showed her parents her slides, many of the scenes were familiar to Kathy from her dreams. Karen, who had never dreamed of her mother before, had dreamed regularly on the tour that her mother was checking with her in person about how it was going. However it happened, they had two lovely trips for the price of one.

There is something deeply touching about the last entry in Dag

Hammarskjöld's book *Markings*,[7] written just before he died in a plane crash. He had written earlier in the book, "A landscape can sing about God. ..." In his last personal entry he told about awakening once again from his recurring dream of a certain land that he had never seen in his waking life. He had been there in different seasons, different light, different weather, and different times of day, but it was the same land. Twice he had climbed on its mountains, stayed by its farthest lake, followed the river toward its source. He concluded:

And I begin to know the map
And to get my bearings.

Then he left this world.

It is easy to understand that these night journeys are gifts to us through the right hemisphere. It is difficult to understand how they could have complex personal meanings. They are perhaps the least psychological of our dreams. Perhaps some of them have no interpretation at all.

Double Meanings

Many dreams can be accurately interpreted in two or more different ways. Arthur Koestler has shared an illustration from his childhood about how a thing can be designed to give two different messages according to which "filter" one uses for perception:

As children we used to be given a curious kind of puzzle to play with. It was a paper with a tangle of very thin blue and red lines. If you just looked at it you couldn't make out anything. But if you covered it with a piece of transparent red tissue-paper, the red lines of the drawing disappeared and the blue lines formed a picture—it was a clown in a circus holding a hoop and a little dog jumping through it. And if you covered the same drawing with blue tissue paper, a roaring lion appeared, chasing the clown across the ring.
Arrival and Departure[8]
Macmillan, 1943

One of the most beautiful dreams I ever had took place near a sunny lagoon. I walked from the sand up a long stairway and came to a door. When I entered, I stepped left and found myself in a room in Holland. It was as orderly, peaceful, and radiant as a painting by Vermeer. I remember a thrilling sense of clarity and snugness, and clean blue and white dishes. I walked out of the room into a garden in Hawaii. I was amazed to realize that Holland, Hawaii, and the United States were joined at this one point. I took a long walk into the damp, earthy, paradise garden among tender green ferns and begonias. I knew I had to return, and so I went through the door and back down the steps to the lagoon to look for the old friend I had left there. Her family heirloom clock and family photo album had been stolen there on the sand, but she was serene about the loss. I took a unique brilliant blue fish from a child who was holding it and set it free in the lagoon where it belonged.

When I look at this dream through Koestler's "red tissue paper" I see the room in Holland representing *The Reformed Journal,* a fine theological periodical with strong ties to Holland, for which I was later to become a contributing editor. I see the Hawaiian garden as representing *The Wittenburg Door,* a very informal and humorous Christian magazine for which I am also a contributing editor. (The latter has nothing to do with Germany, and the men who run it have gone to Hawaii for workshops. I have noticed the editor wearing a string of Hawaiian shells at his neck.)

When I look at the same dream through the "blue tissue paper" I see a completely different meaning. In the dream Holland seemed to be on the left of the stairs and Hawaii seemed to be on the right. My left brain hemisphere is orderly and rational, neat and clear, like the room in my dream. It seems as if dikes hold back the water of the unconscious from my left hemisphere, which is tidy, efficient and productive, cool and controlled. Great waves of the subconscious break upon the shores of my right hemisphere, which is a spatial and intuitive Hawaii represented by the lush, rambling garden in my dream. Unlike Holland Hawaii is volcanic. Fortunately, my mental world brings Holland and Hawaii together.

Without taking time to look at other aspects of this dream, one can see that this one dream travel poster includes two quite different diagrams of reality for my personal life. For well over three years, since that dream, Holland and Hawaii have been personal symbols of certain polarities for me.

Allegories and Romances

In describing two kinds of literature once, C. S. Lewis said, "A strict allegory is like a puzzle with a solution; a great romance is like a flower whose smell reminds you of something you can't quite place."[9] Not all our dreams are one or the other, but some of our most memorable ones are. Two of my many dreams about murder illustrate the difference.

I dreamed this abominable allergory one Sunday morning while my husband was at church. The dream made a memorable sermon. I was alone in a tiny apartment when a young man was murdered nearby during a storm. His body was immediately removed by police, and I entered the apartment to compare it to mine. It was larger and better. I hid in the bathroom and peeked while a big handsome man in a jacket entered and pocketed three bars of gold left by the murder victim. I pretended I did not suspect him of murder or see him take the gold, and we became friends. We went about town together for a long time, always out in public, enjoying lavish foods and beautiful things in style. Then he started asking to borrow money, and I knew he was out of resources. We passed a small group of people in the street, and he told me they were there to deal with quarters. I said I only liked the rich old solid-silver quarters not these tinny substitutes. With that I pulled my gun on him, and he jumped into the river. He was so strong that he soon began to swim upstream and under a wide bridge. I crossed and went into an elegant antique building to finish him. He used to work there and knew it well. Soon he entered and came toward me where I waited in an empty room made of lovely wood. I shot him once in the heart and he fell. As he died in my arms, I told him I hoped he would have a wonderful time.

No one had a flicker of emotion in that dream. The story bothered me after I awakened, and so I tried an imaginary dialogue with elements of the dream. I asked the man why he always wore a jacket, and he grudgingly admitted it was because he was "not very real." Later I learned that his name was Maya or Spirit of the Age. I asked him what the three bars of gold were, and he told me immediately, "Art, music, and literature." (No wonder I went off with him.) I asked why the young man was murdered and knew it was because the Spirit of the Age always takes from the dead past. I saw that, when he stopped enriching me and started to impoverish me, our partnership had to end. He was so strong he could swim either direction in the river of time. I crossed the river on the bridge that spans time, Higher Truth. I entered the building called Culture and finished him off when he tried to win me back. My gun was strong will, and the bullet was hard choice. My last words to him were to wish that he would awaken to a better, more real life. I realized that my dream self was set on always getting better quarters. Although she was no more fully human than a paper doll, being only a symbol of me, she had done right. I asked my dream self her message for me in this strange story. She said "*Keep moving!*"

This allegory was very easy to learn about because I was not in a hurry. I jotted down a couple of answers and then left it for a long time. When I came back, I did that again. If I had tried to force it all at once, it might not have worked. I find that aging of dreams often helps them to reveal themselves. Once I had something very important to write down before I forgot it. I tried to open a beautiful Hawaiian box to get a pen out to write with. I was in a rush and couldn't open the box fast enough. Suddenly the box seemed peculiar, and then it disappeared. When that happened I knew I was dreaming, and that fact awakened me. The important message was gone, and all I had left was the memory of the box I had tried to open too hastily. Perhaps that was an important message in itself. My dreams like to be handled with care.

The following dream is hardly a great romance aesthetically, but in essence it is the story of the greatest romance. It is a "Road to Emmaus" dream; there will be more of them in the final chapter. A group of young criminals came to the mountains in Oregon and lied and killed a healthy old man who rented cabins and bicycles in the wilderness. They beat him on the head. The middle of the dream was not clear. At the end the victim was reviving after all, and the criminals were taken away.

In the middle of the dream there was a young man who told me his name, but I could not remember it after I heard it. I could not remember his face, either, and I don't know what he did. I asked other people, and they said they had the same experience. The name was not hard, but it could not be remembered there. All I could remember was that it started with C, but it was not Chuck. I am always forgetting names in real life, but this name was terribly important. I guessed many, many names, and they were all wrong.

After I awakened, the first name I guessed was Christ. I had not guessed that before, I knew. "Nonsense," I thought, "Christ would not come into such a shoddy, ugly dream as that to set things right." Then it dawned on me. Of course he would.

Notes

1. C. S. Lewis, "The Language of Religion," in *Christian Reflections* (Grand Rapids: Eerdmans, 1967), p. 135.

2. Helen Keller, *The Story of My Life* (New York: Dell, 1961), pp. 404–405.

3. Most of Calvin Hall's essay "Out of a Dream Came the Faucet" is reprinted by Richard M. Jones in *The New Psychology of Dreaming*, pp. 93–95.

4. Duane Schultz, *A History of Modern Psychology* (New York: Academic Press, 1975), p. 123.

5. Thomas De Quincey, "The Dreams of the English Opium-Eater," in *The New World of Dreaming* by Woods and Greenhouse, pp. 60–61.

6. Shirley Motter Linde and Louis M. Savary, *The Sleep Book* (New York: Harper & Row, 1974), p. 50.

7. Dag Hammarskjöld, *Markings* (New York: Knopf, 1964), p. 222.

8. As quoted by Henry Zylstra in *Testament of Vision* (Grand Rapids: Eerdmans, 1958), pp. 125–126.

9. C. S. Lewis in an unpublished letter to Lucy Matthews, available in the Marion E. Wade Collection at Wheaton College, Wheaton, Illinois.

SIX

SEVEN DIALECTS
OF DREAMING:
FREUD TO PROGOFF

Life and dreams are leaves of the same book.

Arthur Schopenhauer, *The World as Will and Idea*

It is commonly known that people who go to Freudian therapists tend to dream with Freudian symbols after awhile, and people who go to Jungian therapists begin to dream about archetypes. Your dreams are apt to conform to expectations. When I was reading Freud once I had a couple of unusual dreams about snakes, and after hearing Patricia Garfield lecture on mandalas I dreamed of visiting a circular island cut into quarters by two intersecting roads. (Only later did I realize that the island was a giant mandala in the sea.) This creative response to suggestion in no way invalidates the dreams so long as we don't apply ready-made interpretations to them.

Following are seven ways of dealing with dreams that are popular today. Although some of the theories flatly contradict others, people who like to be flexible can pick up ideas from all of them for personal use. Just as our styles of dreaming vary, so our styles of dream work will vary. I have illustrated each of these seven methods with dreams from my own diary that seem appropriate.

Freudian Dreams

I have discussed Freudian dream analysis briefly in Chapter 4. I shall demonstrate how it could be used on three of my dreams.

I dreamed I husked an ear of corn that my husband had bought, and the cob inside had no edible corn on it. "A bad ear!" I was thinking as I awoke. How did this dream incorporate recent memories? We had indeed been fixing fresh corn on the cob frequently, and I had in fact been suffering pain in one of my ears, caused by a sore throat. Is there a pun in the dream? There is a double pun. First, I used an ear of corn to comment upon the pain in my own ear. Second, I'm sure I did that to illustrate my opinion that dream puns are corny. In my opinion such witticisms are fun for fun's sake. But Freud said that both parapraxes [slips of the tongue] and wit are symptomatic behavior which must be subjected to careful examination and interpretation.[1] I suppose he would find obvious penis envy in this dream.

One night in my sleep I read a long poem praising and fostering harmony and peace. The man who wrote it was describing a certain family fight in order to moralize about good normative family values. The last two lines, all I could recall after awakening, were:

The children are enraged because their gifts aren't from above,
And the parents are enraged because they don't know how to love.

The startling contrast between the alleged content of the poem and the unresolved family rage actually expressed in its conclusion might strike students of Freud as an indication that there is terrific repressed hostility in this dreamer, probably because of unfulfilled infantile wishes for more direct expressions of parental love.

In another dream I read an extremely long first-person article in *Guideposts* magazine. It told of a woman who returned from Europe to visit her widowed mother and was tricked into staying with her. The mother was a tidy little lady. When the grown daughter lost her temper, her mother made her do behavior exercises before a mirror. The daughter found a mandrake root and met an important Jewish man named Abraham. Then the mother and daughter had a disagreement and the mother hissed a series of vile imprecations, including, "I'll be the snot that drips from the spout of the teapot of God for you!" The daughter fled to Abraham. At that point my son awakened me, and I didn't get to finish the *Guideposts* article. A Freudian might note immediately that a post (even a guidepost) is a phallic symbol and that Abraham is a traditional father figure as well as the prototype of all who are called to leave their homeland. A mandrake root is a potent narcotic traditionally thought to be sexually arousing. This bizarre tale presented innocently to the dreamer as an uplifting true story in a wholesome inspirational magazine would, I assume, cause students of Freud to suspect a repressed Electra complex— the female equivalent of an Oedipus complex. In her unconscious the dreamer-reader still wants to displace her mother as the sexual lover of her father.

Jungian Dreams

I discussed Jung's approach to dreams briefly in Chapter 4. Very appropriate to his theory was a 1975 dream in which I discovered that I have a wise woman psychologist who goes everywhere with me and understands everything, even things I do not notice. I suppose she understands all my dreams immediately.

Jung might have appreciated the following pair of dreams, the first being a preface and aid to interpretation for the second. In real life our friends the Barrets were taking us to the Music Center in Los Angeles to celebrate our anniversary. That morning I dreamed that the show at the Center was going to be Episcopalian and that John and I would be on television. We would be highly honored by getting to see three important Episcopalian symbols— the star, the cross, and the crown. It occurred to me that this was all closely connected somehow with Robert Browning's title *The Ring and the Book,* in fact, a work I have never read.

In the next dream I found myself with an anonymous man who had a tubular cannister, shaped like a picture light, hanging around his neck. It reminded me of a phylactery in which a Jewish male would keep a Scripture passage. It was made of certain silver and gold-colored metal, and it was really an unbreakable glasscase. I complimented the man on his high-quality glasscase, and he gladly told me that this was the "Christian Faith" brand of sunglasses. I thought that sounded peculiar, to say the least. He said this brand came in three style: Ezekiel, Paul, and John of Patmos. This set of three biblical names meant nothing special to me at the time. He hadn't wanted the Ezekiel style, he said, because it was too narrow for him. He had chosen the John style, which was so popular that he had a very hard time finding any. He tried them on for me, and I told him they looked wonderful on him. I noticed that they were not dark glasses after all. The glass was clear and the frame was gold-colored metal. I told him warmly that he looked perfect in these glasses. He was so pleased that he put his hand on my shoulder and then kissed me on my cheek.

At this point my husband John said, "Would you like to get up?" I realized he had just touched my shoulder and kissed my cheek. I immediately recorded four different dreams on cassette tape, the last one first, and wondered if this last one would have become more significant if it had not been interrupted. About two weeks later I recalled this dream when a store we shop in featured some new picture frames made out of the very metal that the dream frames and case had been composed of. I recognized it instantly. I went back to the dream to see what was there.

Looking for wordplay in addition to the metal frames for glasses and pictures, I hoped that sunglasses would not be a religious pun, Son-glasses. But ultimately that had to be. The theme was vision, because Ezekiel, Paul and John of Patmos are, I realized, the three most prominent visionaries in the Bible in my opinion. The man in the dream had his glasses for vision not protection.

When I asked what silver and gold mean to me, two things popped into my mind. First, a lame man was begging at the

Beautiful Gate of the temple in Jerusalem and *saw* Peter and John entering, as recorded in Acts 3. Peter *looked* at the man, with John, and directed him to *fix his eyes* upon them. He *looked* right at them, expecting some money. Peter then said, "No silver and gold have I, but what I do have I will give you. In the name of Jesus of Nazareth start walking." (v.6; Williams). That is one of my favorite stories in the entire Bible. Second, I learned a rhyme when I was a child that has always stayed with me:

Make new friends, but keep the old;
One is silver and the other is gold.

Because of that rhyme gold and silver have always meant old and new to me. Obviously the gold and silver glasscase is the Bible, made up of the Old and New Testaments. The message it contains enables people to see Jesus Christ of Nazareth and to be healed.

This made me very curious about who the man was who touched me and kissed me just as my husband did to wake me up. I felt silly when it finally dawned upon me; the man was my husband, of course. The dream meant to finish that way. No wonder I had dreamed earlier that John and I were to be on television together and see three Episcopalian symbols. The star, a symbol of prophecy, signified Ezekiel's vision. The cross, a symbol of suffering servanthood, signified Paul's vision. The crown, a symbol of heaven, signified John's vision. John's vision was John's vision in this case. It is true that my husband has a new outlook on life recently. He agreed with my dream when I shared it with him. What did all this have to do with the words "the ring and the book"? We were celebrating our anniversary, and I saw a wedding band on a Bible in my mind. According to the preface, this religious symbolism was all at the Center. That was a symbol too.[2]

Shortly before this Christian sunglasses festival of symbols, I had a related dream that was very simple. I suddenly learned that I have never raised the shades in my study to the top of the windows because the windows go higher than I thought. "Let the shades go to the top of the page!" I said, as if my sunlight poured in through a book every day. The idea of increased light in my study filled me with excitement and joy.

Two years earlier I had dreamed of arriving at a tiny frame house in a dusty, dingy countryside. I entered and found that the back wall of the house was solid window, overlooking a gigantic landscape of columns of red rock in radiant sunlight, so beautiful that I was overwhelmed and stunned by joy. These two dreams are like the many dreams that some of us have had about suddenly discovering splendid new rooms at the back of our house or a whole new story upstairs or a valuable expanse of new land in our back yard. To Jung these dreams are good signs of personal growth.

Dreams can be bad signs also. Hitler was asleep in a bunker during World War I and dreamed that the dirt was caving in on him and his fellow soldiers, strangling and crushing them. He jumped up and ran out on the field, in his alarm, just as an explosion buried all the rest of his group alive in the bunker. Hitler used that prophetic dream to bolster his idea that he was destined to rule the world. Laurens van der Post says that Hitler misread the language of his dream. It was warning him that he was being buried alive in spiritual dirt in his unconscious mind, and he did not heed the warning.

Adlerian Dreams

Alfred Adler was not consistent in his approach to dreams, sometimes considering them evidence of lack of a common-sense approach to life. He wrote once, "The purpose of dreams must be in the feelings they arouse."[3] Adler was largely concerned with people's feelings of inadequacy.

Adler noted the frequency with which people dream of coming to a test totally unprepared or being late to class. Pauline Baynes, the English artist, told me that for many years she had bad nightmares about being late to class, left over from her school days. I still have them, usually set in the junior high school I attended. They have progressed to the point where I don't know my schedule, have no locker, and can't even find the office. My running footsteps echo up and down the halls and stairways while classes are in progress, and somewhere, behind one of the closed doors, I am being marked absent. I used to have dreams every August about appearing to teach high school, only to find myself partially naked in the classroom. I began asking fellow teachers if they had ever heard of such a thing, and most of those I asked said that they had the same or similar bad dreams in August, even if they had no conscious anxiety about coping with classes in September.

One day I received a spring book catalog with a two-page spread in it announcing my first book. That night I dreamed I put on a new style of eye makeup. To my surprise it made me black from my lashes to my eyebrow—black as ink. That may be someone's idea of fashion, I thought, but it doesn't suit me at all! Although I was not well experienced in dream analysis then, I figured that the "eye in black ink" could symbolize the "I in print." Did this mean that the delightful prospect of appearing in print was somehow unpleasant? I don't want to look peculiar to people by writing books. I don't want to give myself a black eye. When I tried out those phrases on myself, they clicked. Both the feeling and the illustration seemed absurd, but I realized they were a tiny part of me that I had not been aware of. Later I realized that such anxiety about people's reactions is not wholly inappropriate.

Gestalt Dreams

Carl Jung was the first to suggest conversing with dream elements while reflecting upon dreams. Fritz Perls, the founder of Gestalt therapy, capitalized upon that idea.[4] He taught that every aspect of a dream is a creation of the dreamer and that every aspect represents a part of the dreamer here and now. Freud called dreams the Royal Road to the unconscious, but Perls said they are the Royal Road to the integration of the many parts of our personalities. *Gestalt* is a German word meaning the whole pattern with all its parts in place.

Perls advised us not to interpret dreams but to relive them in the present tense, dramatically bringing them back to life. "Just take any old dream or dream fragment," he said casually, because they are all so rich in insights. He suggested writing the dream down in detail, then taking the role of each person or thing and speaking out for it. Let the elements that oppose each other have a dialogue. Switching from one chair to another for the different identities is very helpful. The opposing entities are often in serious conflict with each other, and letting them resolve their differences in waking dream dialogue can release blocked energy in real life. Perls found that the conflict is often between a self-righteous "topdog" and a whiney "underdog" in the personality. The topdog is overly demanding, and the underdog is sneaky and weak. They both need transformation.

Perls warned that dreamers who have no living beings in their dreams are apt to be seriously mentally ill and need professional help. People who do not recall any dreams are often just afraid to cope with them because they want to think they have everything well controlled. Those people can often converse with their missing dreams successfully by letting the dreams answer questions such as "Dreams, where are you?" Dreamers can try asking questions like "Dreams, why don't you give me more pleasure?" Some temperament types find that these Perls dialogues flow surprisingly easily (they must not be planned). Perls says that if you do Gestalt dream work with other people they will keep you more alert and honest.

Once I had a very "Perlsian" dream. My mother was nagging and pressuring me to do a million and one things right away. I blew up at her. "You want to be me, but you can't. I am I. I want to try to be *I* right *here* in this *place* right *now* at this *time!* Quit pushing me! Here and now! Do you understand?" I was screaming hysterically. John came in and looked at me with mild disapproval. I turned to him for protection from my mother and control of my tantrum. This dream is almost ludicrous in that it fit Gestalt therapy so well before I knew that technique. I could use three chairs to work out this inner battle: one for the unreasonable topdog, one for the weak and furious underdog, and one for the fair-minded observer who sees the "torture game" the other two are playing. All are within.

Later I had one of those embarrassing dreams that can make us feel mortified when we awaken. I was at a *Wittenburg Door* meeting in our usual restaurant in San Diego, but I was snuggling up to publisher Mike Yaconelli, who had his arm around my shoulder. We were openly expressing immense affection for each other.

It occurred to me that his wife would not understand if she found out. Then we were all at a beautiful upstairs apartment, and I had to give a brief report, which was worthless and stupid; when I sat back down, I saw that I was wearing dreadful clothes. Then I learned that our editor Denny Rydberg had stepped into the kitchen to prepare us a magnificent dinner almost instantly, as if by magic. I could already smell the odors of roast beef and brewed coffee.

Trying the Gestalt method later, I asked "Mike" what part of me he was, and he answered simply, "I love you." That gave me a delicious feeling. When I think about the real Mike, I have the impression that he has great concern for the welfare of his family and the church at large. I saw that Mike is the part of me most concerned about my spouse, my children, and the church, and that part of me really loves the rest of me instead of judging me harshly as a topdog would do. It was obvious that my stupid, ugly self at the meeting is my "not-OK" self, but she is tolerated and does not have to resort to underdog behavior. The new apartment let me know it is an "upper room" part of me, a sacred meeting place for personality elements, happy to be of service. As Denny went by in my recreated dream, I asked him who he was and he didn't answer. Luckily, I was firm and asked again. He turned and said impersonally, "I am the one who brought you here." In real life he summoned me to editorial meetings and managed them, and here he had been my inner dream editor! My own conviction is that his cooking us all a sublime dinner was a picture of Shakespeare's tribute to the sleeping mind—"Chief nourisher in life's feast." The Mike in me wants to nurture others, and the Denny in me nurtures me; and in this dream we are happily integrated as soon as I accept all three parts as cooperative parts of me with contrasting styles and functions.

Over two years later I dreamed that the same staff was meeting informally at night in the old garage by the alley behind my childhood home, where many of my strangest dreams still take place. I was sitting with a young man in the back yard earnestly listening to his plan to start a new ministry—a chapel for dogs. As he tried to tell me his plans, we were repeatedly drowned out by the howling and barking of neighborhood dogs. I walked into the garage and asked Denny and his colleagues who were standing there what they were laughing at, but they wouldn't explain what their joke was. All I knew was that it was a "standing joke." Later I rode off with them in Denny's sporty car to continue the dream meeting elsewhere. I was telling Denny how incredibly shoddy the houses were that he was taking us past, and at that point he drove past one that was incredibly splendid. It filled me with joy. It had a gigantic sparkling green statue of Santa Claus in the front yard. The dream ended when Denny indicated that he couldn't find a parking place, and I was still wondering what the joke had been.

After I awakened, it was quite awhile before I realized that my inner Denny had orchestrated all the dog racket to point out that a chapel for dogs had to be a racket; I never suspected at the time that the young man was a fraud or that the unusual barking was a kind of fraud also. (There are no dogs in that neighborhood in real life.) As a continuation of that earlier dream of Denny as dream editor, this one indicates that he puts the humor in on purpose and enjoys it. He seems to be like the stage manager of an impromptu play who sometimes takes a minor role himself.

Five months later, in the October 10, 1978, issue of *Sources and Resources,* I discovered the headline "Is Your Puppy Born Again?" That is the first time I ever encountered the subject in waking life. (*Sources and Resources* was another publication edited by Denny Rydberg.) The very next day I received a note from Dr. Lewis Smedes, Professor of Christian Ethics at Fuller Theological Seminary, telling me—out of the blue—that he had a bad dream about being unable to minister adequately to a suffering dog. His dream was indeed memorable, and I thought that Gestalt was one of the techniques worth trying on it.

Incidentally, the real Denny Rydberg is not overly humorous and my dream life is not overly humorous. I had thought my dream life was almost all happy in recent years. In one dream I read several articles in *Human Behavior* magazine, including a research report pointing out that there are as many tragedies as comedies but that people assume there are more comedies because they pay more attention to the comedies. Suspecting that I was the "people" in the survey, I guessed that this was a commentary on dream life. I checked over my dream diary to see if the report was true. It was. There were far more sad or frightening dreams than I would have guessed.

Senoi Dreams

The dream theories and practice that reportedly came to us from a tribe in Malaysia will be discussed in Chapter 7. In short, this theory urges us to confront the elements in our dreams assertively while we are dreaming, knowing that they cannot overcome us and can bless us.

When C. S. Lewis was a child, he was haunted by dreams of giant insects. My worst dreams have been of worms, caterpillars, snails, and slugs. (The last time I dreamed of them, fairly recently, they were writhing all over my front walk on a thick layer of bacon grease, trying to eat each other up.) When my husband was a boy, he was chased by dream bears at night until he could find a cliff or high building to jump from in order to wake up or die.

Our first son was chased by dream wolves all the time until I first read about the Senoi in 1969. I immediately assured my son that it is good to dream about wolves because you can easily fight the whole pack and beat them. I encourage him vividly and repeatedly. One morning his bedclothes were all in a tangle, and he reported that he beat the wolves. I suspected that he was fooling. It happened several more times, however, and then the wolves never came back!

I know an American woman who developed this technique on her own when she was eight years old. She suffered childhood nightmares about fire and falling. She decided that in fire nightmares she would produce hoses to put out fires, and in falling nightmares she would produce umbrellas to parachute to safety. It worked, and the nightmares went away. As a young mother she began to have nightmares about nuclear attacks from Russia from which she wanted to protect her children. She decided that if Russia attacks there is nothing better to do than to watch the show before dying, so in future nightmares of that kind she would take her children up on the roof to watch the bombs arrive. They did that a few times in her dreams, and then the Russians stopped attacking. She used to assume that everyone knew enough to handle nightmares that way.

In contrast, a man who lived to eighty-three suffered the same nightmare frequently in his childhood and less frequently in adulthood until in his last years it only came once or twice a year. But it came with a vengeance. In the dream he would be alone in any room, and an ordinary animal like a cat or dog would stand in the doorway, then grow immense, with ferocious eyes, blocking his only means of escape. His terror was so great that he would sometimes throw himself off his bed. He would kick, struggle, and tremble violently. Once after surgery in his last years he tore out all his stitches by thrashing in an agony of terror even after he had been awakened. He was a kindly and sensible man who led a gentle and placid life. One wonders if seventy-odd years of repeated nightmares could have been avoided for him by a simple plan of attack against the doorway animals.

A popular adaptation of Senoi dream work in the United States now applies the Senoi techniques to past dreams through recall. I attended a Senoi dream workshop in which the leader used a recent dream of mine that I had not thought about at all. I was to tell it in the present tense with my eyes closed. "I find myself in a large house that, to my surprise, we are moving into. I am very uneasy because I can't imagine living there. We won't have enough furniture. The current owner has a huge metal bread-making machine in the living room with dough in it. I wish I did not have to spend my time making bread here. The living room walls are almost all glass, so there is no feeling of privacy, and the lighting and decor are bleak. The roof is extremely high, supported by massive beams that swoop up from the floor and meet overhead. The dining room walls are papered with two clashing designs—a patriotic motif and a Raggedy Ann and Andy pattern."

I couldn't help knowing that this was a typical dream about shifting lifestyles. I came to realize later that the bread machine symbolized concern about money making and that the incongruous wallpapers represented public service clashing with informal private family living (because Ann is my middle name and I keep Raggedy Ann and Andy dolls in my bedroom). But the Senoi method involves experience rather than interpretation.

Our leader asked me to name the most powerful figure, which was the house and its beams, and to make it an ally of mine by asking what gift it wanted from me. The great beams seemed to reply that they wanted warmth and humanity in the house. Because one can transform anything in dreams, I redecorated the dining room and living room, throwing out the bread machine and bringing in colorful furnishings and art and music that provide warmth and joy. Then I was to ask for a gift that revealed the essence of friendship and power. To my surprise, the beams seemed to give me from their essence a wooden cross that could fit into my hand. Then I was told to open my eyes and draw a picture of the gift and to keep the picture in sight at home as a reminder. I still have that sketch of a cross where I can see it. I value it.

There are two modifications to this technique. If the main figure is hostile and won't cooperate, tell it to take off its mask and assume its real form. Do that until it has a "face" you can deal with. Don't give it anything you don't want to give. Second, if the gift you receive does not express friendship and power to you, ask for another or transform it yourself. The basis of Senoi dream work is assertiveness and receiving gifts.

Feeling Therapy Dreams

Feeling Therapy is the first dream theory to reach the public through appearances of its founders on television talk shows. They have founded a community in Los Angeles.[5] Feeling Therapists, according to their publicity, have created a new lifestyle with a "supersonic dimension of feeling." They warn that it is dangerous to dabble with your dreams and feelings unless we do it with their guidance. "Dreams should not be controlled, manipulated, interpreted, or understood from an intellectual place," accordimg to one team member.

Dreams work against us if we fail to pay attention to them. But paying attention to normal dreams won't work because they require interpretation, and dream interpretation is not the answer. The answer is to discover "Breakthru Dreams" and to meet the "Dream Maker." They liken this meeting to a good LSD trip. A

Dream Maker lives in all of us and wants to live more fully. If our dreams are things that just happen to us, they come to us from the Dream Maker within but are censored. If we feel and move and express ourselves in our dreams, then we are one with the Dream Maker. If we live our feelings fully, we can all become Dream Makers. That will cure us of our terrific numbness and isolation. People who become Dream Makers can recognize each other, but other people cannot recognize them.

If we are willing to live intensely, we will have many Breakthru Dreams. The five elements needed in balanced abundance in any Breakthru Dream are expression, feeling, clarity, contact, and activity. The two important things to do with dreams afterward are to focus on how the dream feels and to talk to people about it that day. Talking about dream feelings is paramount, which means that a supportive community is essential. Feeling is much more important than thought in the new age. The initial Breakthru Dream is preceded by waking distress or possible mental disturbance of brief duration and it comes as a nightmare, but later Breakthru Dreams may be pleasant.

Once I dreamed that my little son Peter had fallen into a round narrow hole in the ground and was caught. Alarmed, I pressed gently on one side of the hole and tilted it over sideways so he could crawl out unharmed. Success! I was told in the dream that this unusual scene was so good that it had been photographed for inclusion in an old silent comedy made many years before it happened. Amused by the way I had manipulated space, matter, and time, I told the dream to my husband the next day. This would rate as a dream that worked fairly well by Dream Maker standards because (1) I had some feelings, (2) I was very active, (3) the dream was vivid, (4) I was the star performer, (5) I included a friend in the dream, (6) I told someone about the dream.

A special dream I had five years ago is still vividly emotional for me. I entered a house through an opening so low that I had to crawl in. It was exactly like a cave entrance, but down inside was a perfectly beautiful home, and I realized that I was the lovely homemaker. The feeling there was waves of serene bliss. My wonderful husband, Dr. Prince, arrived home from work and watched me as I dealt with a female relative of his who was there to give her daughter to him, to my surprise. I took the unwanted child on my lap affectionately and asked her age, which was ten. Her face was a mass of pimples, but I held her and talked to her in a wonderful way.

Upon reflection, I realized that my personal world had collapsed when I was ten years old. I actually know of a charming Dr. Prince who has the outstanding trait of telling his patients in detail what is going on inside them instead of assuming that they couldn't understand or that they should not know. When he treated me once, he caused me to feel brief but intense physical pain and made me well. In every way, this would seem to be an excellent Feeling Therapy dream. It was radiant and deeply moving, I was in charge and active, and Dr. Prince, who owned the beautiful home and let me run it my way, obviously manifested the Dream Maker himself. The dream made me feel refreshed and happy in my waking life and still does when I think about it.

However, this dream doesn't count for much in Breakthru Dream terms because the Feeling Therapists had not yet developed their system for achieving dreams like this one at that time, and I dreamed it independently rather than within their extended community. The Feeling Therapists recognize themselves as a modern manifestation of the ancient tradition of shamans and witch doctors in primitive tribes, with belief in the supernatural replaced by belief in powerful "inner processes." I asked one of them how they account for precognitive dreams in their system, and he answered frankly that they do not have some of these questions figured out yet. The highest value in this form of community therapy is feeling more and feeling better. It seems to be geared especially to rootless young adults who lack deep personal relationships and are out of touch with their feelings.

Intensive Journal Dreams

Depth-psychologist Ira Progoff's approach to dreams is in a sense the most original one at this time. It is a part of the Intensive Journal Experience that he has developed, based upon the belief that all the relationships and events in our lives have a purpose and work together as we move in our own direction. The Journal

Experience, which Progoff and his affiliates teach in workshops across the country, reveals that life pattern to a person. A lifelong dream record is part of the journal. The dreams express much conscious material, but they also show what deeper-than-conscious goals are seeking to unfold.

The journal writer goes back as far as possible in memory and records all the dreams or fragments of dreams found there, in the order of their history. A current dream log is kept as well. There is to be no interpretation, only reliving. The writer rereads all the dreams repeatedly and reflects upon their movement, tone, and feeling. Nightmares should be included and considered tunnels we go through on our journey toward our destination. Everything leads toward the goal and meaning of this life. "It is in order that we may get these messages of inner guidance from the depth of ourselves that we pay attention to our dreams."[6]

At certain stages along the way you sit in quietness working in depth with your dreams according to methods in the Intensive Journal. Then you are ready for a *life correlation* process. In this experience you have already gained a new image of your conscious life. Sitting quietly, you "hold" that in your right hand, which is controlled by the rational left hemisphere of the brain. In your left hand you "hold" the new image you have of the unified movement of your inner unconscious life, which relates to the intuitive right hemisphere of the brain. Weigh the two; feel them come into balance. Bring them together and be receptive to whatever they communicate to each other or to you. New understanding will come. The inner life is being balanced. Needless to say, only expert leadership makes such a mystical-sounding experience possible to ordinary people. That is the nature of Progoff's work.

Because of Ira Progoff's advice, I started to record any childhood dreams I could recall. That caused others to occasionally come to mind. The two earliest that I have now recalled came as memories that deeply moved me. The earliest, when I was about three, was that two empty chairs on a front porch where I stood started to rock, although I could see no one there. My parents did not believe in the supernatural and I had few contacts with anyone else, being an only child out in the country unexposed to radio or television. I can't imagine where I got the idea of spirits, but I somehow knew I was in the presence of spirits and was terrified. I never got over the shock of the reality of invisible presences in that dream.

The second childhood dream I know of happened when I was kindergarten age. I was in the home of a poor little girl I knew, and a black and white film was showing on a screen in her living room. I had never seen a home movie or television, and so this was strange in itself. The movie showed a flood. The next thing I knew, I was up on the screen in the movie myself, being swept away by what seemed a very real flood. I puzzled for weeks afterward about what it could mean to have a movie of a flood in a humble home, and what it could mean to become a person in that movie. Now I know.

I have had a series of flood, tidal-wave, and deep-water dreams ever since then. As a child I would usually be on the sand trying to run in helpless terror. Later I was often in houses that were totally submerged or soon would be. As an adult I am often in a house on a cliff that is being inundated. In one dream I walked out of a dormitory in rain boots to mail a letter just before the battered cliff collapsed into the sea—mail box, dormitory, boots, and all. In another, Professor Clinton McLemore, author of *Clergyman's Psychological Handbook*, was taking me for a drive and pulled over to the edge of a high cliff to give me a view of the ocean. "I'm sorry the water is so far below us," he said. I told him the ocean was plenty close enough, because the waves were up to the top of the cliff. Just then foam splashed across the road. (That's the only time I ever had a psychologist along when the waves got out of hand.) The best tidal-wave dream I ever had was the time I decided I might as well enjoy it as I died. I threw myself in, and after ages of swirling and tumbling I came out on top of the mountain of water feeling exultant. I had not needed to breathe after all. In the Intensive Journal experience one relives all this private mythology.

An individual dream of mine that I suspect of expressing my life movement, although I do not understand it, involved a pure white bird on my shoulder that I loved and revered. A large black cat approached with malice. I gave the bird a light toss so it would

soar out of danger. Instead, for some reason it sank, and the
panther-cat was at it instantly. I awakened fighting to save the
bird even if it cost me my life.

Such dreams are part of the basic memories of our lives, according to Progoff. If we use the Intensive Journal technique, our
dreams will, all together, guide us on our life journey.

Chanticleer's Dream

One of the finest and silliest dream accounts in literature is found
in Chaucer's *Canterbury Tales,* written around 1400. His "Nun's
Priest's Tale" is about the love life, dream life, pride, and wit of
the chickens belonging to a poor widow. The widow had a glorious golden rooster named Chanticleer, who was quite a philosopher. He had seven fine hens in his harem, including his beautiful
wife Pertelote, whom he loved ardently since she was a very
young chicken.

One morning before sunrise Chanticleer started groaning like a
man with bad dreams. Pertelote asked, "Dear heart, what ails you
to groan this way?"

"Madam," Chanticleer replied, "I pray you are not upset. By
God, I dreamed I was in such mischief just now, that my heart is
still sore afraid. Now God interpret my dream right and keep me
out of foul captivity!" (The word foul may be a pun here. Foul
and fowl coexisted in Chaucer's Middle English.)

Chanticleer told his wife that in his dream a strange animal
appeared in the farmyard to kill him and eat him. His eloquent
description makes it clear that the unfamiliar animal was really a
fox. Pertelote scolded Chanticleer for being a foolish coward:

Alas! and can you be afraid of dreams?
God knows that they're no more than silly scenes!

Pertelote gave Chanticleer a stern lecture about how dreams are
caused by upsets in the body and how she planned to cure him
with herbs. Then she lectured him on herbs. (Her diagnosis and
prescriptions were authoritative in Chaucer's day.) She quoted the
Roman moralist Cato to prove her point about dreams:

I'll pass on as lightly as I can.
Lo, Cato, who was such a wise man,
Didn't he say, "Don't bother with dreams?"
Now sire, when we fly down from the beams
For God's sake, take some laxative.
Upon my soul and as I live
I counsel you wisely. . . .

Chanticleer thanked her at the end of her speech, but he claimed that many writers with more authority than Cato say just the opposite about dreams. Then he lectured her in verse about the significance of dreams, with examples from Greek history and the Bible and other sources, even quoting Latin to her and purposely fooling her about the translation:

Briefly I'll say, for my conclusion
That this warning dream was no delusion
And I will add, furthermore,
That in laxatives I set no store
For they are toxic, I know good and well;
I trust them less than words can tell.

However, it was such a beautiful spring day and Chanticleer was so much in love with Pertelote and life in general that he decided to disregard his fearful dream entirely. Needless to say, there is lot more to this story, and a real fox almost succeeds in eating Chanticleer, which proves that the elegant, eloquent cock was right and the hen was wrong this time. Chaucer worked in plenty of adult humor about male-female relationships.

Chanticleer and Pertelote represented the first two of the three most prevalent attitudes toward dreams in 1400: (1) All dreams are meaningless results of our physical condition; (2) some dreams are truly prophetic; (3) some dreams are demonic. (Pertelote could have told Chanticleer to pray for protection against night demons that torment sleepers.)

Today skeptical Pertelote might have taken a know-it-all Freudian, Jungian, Adlerian, Gestalt, Senoi, Feeling Therapy, or Intensive Journal approach to her husband's bad dream. If Pertelote was a Freudian, she might have told the cock:

This is a secret sexual wish,
To end up in a strange beast's dish.
The beast is your mother; you want again
To enter an egg inside that hen.

If Pertelote were a follower of Jung, she might have told Chanticleer:

The doglike beast I know full well,
For he is called the Hound of Hell.
Your dream is neither truth nor tripe—
You met a major Archetype!

If Pertelote followed Adler, she might have said:

You rule the farm with poultry power,
Calling out the passing hour,
All golden on the garden gate;
You fear to lose your high estate.

If Pertelote were delving into Gestalt, she might have said:

The beast is just one part of you,
So ask him what he wants to do.
You'll understand him, I allow—
Topdog/underdog, here and now!

If Pertelote knew Senoi dream theory, she could say:

Congratulations, feathered one!
Next time you see that beast, don't run.
Attack and conquer him, dear cock,
And get a gift for all your flock.

If Pertelote believed in Feeling Therapy, she could say:

It's clear that you are out of touch
With what you feel. It isn't much
To see a stranger wanting you
And somehow failing to get through.

If, however, Pertelote followed Intensive Journal ideas, she might say:

Record the dream in chicken scratches;
An egg cracked open never hatches.
So let it be, if you are wise.
Observe the beast; don't analyze!

Chaucer's *Book of the Duchess, House of Fame, Parliament of Fowls,* and *Legend of Good Women* all mention that they came to him in dreams. That is probably just the traditional literary device used by John Bunyan in *Pilgrim's Progress,* C. S. Lewis in *Pilgrim's Regress* and *The Great Divorce,* and many other authors over the centuries. But the poems themselves show that Chaucer took a genuine interest in the dream experience. As a sophisticated Englishman with high connections in the late 1300s, he could easily have taken Pertelote's popular position, which was to prevail for centuries among educated Christians. Instead, Chaucer looked into other sources to learn more about dreams.

Actually, recent research shows that chickens don't have REM dreaming after their first few days of life. But if Chanticleer was groaning in his dream, he could have been having a deep sleep nightmare anyway.

Chaucer ended the story of Chanticleer and Pertelote piously:

But you that hold this tale to be folly
As of a fox, or of a cock and hen,
Take the moral of it, good men.
For St. Paul says that all good writing
Is surely in some way enlightening;
Take the fruit, and let the husk lie still.

It sounds like a good rule for dream work.

Notes

1. Robert M. Goldensen, *The Encyclopedia of Human Behavior* (Garden City, New York: Doubleday, 1970), p. 1048.
2. "Deep within us all there is an amazing inner sanctuary of the soul, a holy place, a Divine Center, a speaking voice, to which we may continuously return." Thomas R. Kelly, *A Testament of Devotion* (New York: Harper & Brothers, 1941), p. 29.

3. Alfred Adler, "Dreams Reveal the Life Style" in *The New World of Dreams* by Woods and Greenhouse, p. 213.

4. Frederick S. Perls, *Gestalt Therapy Verbatim* (Moab, Utah: Real People Press, 1969).

5. See Richard Corriere and Joseph Hart, *The Dream Makers* (New York: Funk and Wagnalls, 1977). Their first book, describing what they call perhaps the most incredible discovery since Freud's discovery of the unconscious is *Going Sane: An Introduction to Feeling Therapy* by Joseph Hart, Richard Corriere, and Jerry Binder (New York: Jason Aronson, 1975).

6. Ira Progoff, "Working with our Dreams," *At a Journal Workshop* (New York: Dialogue House Library, 1975), p. 244.

SEVEN

EDEN SPOILED:
WHOSE FOOL ARE YOU?

The woods are made for the hunters of dreams,
The brooks for the fishers of song....

Sam Walter Foss, *The Bloodless Sportsman*

Forgers of Dreams and Fishers of Song

We can get fooled when we are dreaming, we can dream that we
are fooled, and we can get fooled about someone else dreaming.
Fools dream dreams, dreams fool fools, and even the wisest person
can be tricked one way or another.

Thomas Babington Macauley was a brilliant author-historian
of the last century. Fortunately for Macauley, the notorious diary
that Londoner Samuel Pepys wrote in code in the 1660s came to
light in time for Macauley to make good professional use of it; he
was an expert on that bit of history.

Macauley loved young people. He had a niece named Alice,
who one night came to Macauley in a vivid dream, remorse all

over her face. She confessed to him that the Pepys diary—which he and other scholars had been using—was all a forgery and that she was the person who had forged it.

"What!" Macauley exclaimed. "I have been quoting in reviews, and in my *History,* a forgery of yours as a book of highest authority. How shall I ever hold up my head again?"

He awoke with the horror of the idea, poor Alice's pleading voice still in his ears. Afterward, his relief and amusement were so great that he told the dream in a letter to a friend with great relish. By dreaming that he had been fooled, Macauley was briefly fooled about being fooled by his own dream. He enjoyed the joke.[1]

Niels Bohr did not enjoy an extremely different kind of dream fiction, which occurred a century later. Bohr is a Nobel Prize-winning physicist. As the story has been repeated from book to book and in magazines, Bohr was still a student when he dreamed one night that he was on a sun composed of burning gas. Planets whistled by, attached to the sun by thin filaments. All cooled and solidified and crumbled away. Bohr realized that he had conceived a model of the atom. This is how he came to think of the atom as a nucleus with electrons revolving around it. This was a breakthrough in modern physics.

It is a lovely story, and the only trouble with it is that it is not true. When sleep expert William Dement asked about it, Bohr denied it all and said that he has never got any usable idea from a dream in his life. Furthermore, he said, he was not the originator of the planetary model of the atom in the first place.

Niels Bohr may never have got any food for thought from a dream, but we are told on good authority that some people in the Gilbert Islands used to get food for the body from dreams. This far-fetched story would hardly be worth considering except that it was witnessed and told by Sir Arthur Grimble of the British Colonial Service, a highly credible man. In 1918 he went out to the Gilbert Islands as an administrator who had affection and respect for the islanders. He served so well that in 1938 he was knighted. His two books about his adventures there, *We Chose the Islands* and *Return to the Islands,* appeared in the 1950s to good reviews.

One of the many stories Grimble told was "the calling of the porpoises." He had been advised to eat porpoise meat to put on weight, and a helpful islander took him to Kuma village where the hereditary porpoise callers lived. The best caller greeted Grimble when he arrived, then retired to his hut to sleep and dream while everyone waited for the feast. In his special dream (in which he believed his spirit traveled out of his body) he located the porpoise-folk far out at sea and invited them to a dance, with feasting, at Kuma. The porpoises followed him to the ocean surface with porpoise cries of joy, then headed toward Kuma. Gilbert watched the villagers greet the porpoises at the shore as they arrived after the dream, dozens and dozens drifting in to the villagers in neat rows. The leader swam right to the dreamer himself, who walked it to the edge of the water and lifted it up onto the sand. The other villagers crooned to the other porpoises as they did the same. The porpoises seemed to want only to go ashore with the humans. There they were slaughtered and eaten.

There is an uncanny resemblance between Grimble's account of dreaming the porpoises in to shore and Lewis Carroll's famous account of an oyster feast called "The Walrus and the Carpenter" in *Through the Looking Glass.* Could Carroll have hit upon aspects of the South Seas phenomenon by intuition? Could Grimble have constructed his porpoise tale from childhood memories of "The Walrus and the Carpenter"? Could the similarity be coincidental? Every option seems far-fetched. The key stanzas that tell Carroll's story of the oysters follow:

"O Oysters, come and walk with us!"
   The Walrus did beseech.
"A pleasant walk, a pleasant talk,
   Along the briny beach.... "

... Four young oysters hurried up,
   All eager for the treat:
Their coats were brushed, their faces washed,
   Their shoes were clean and neat—
And this was odd, because you know,
   They hadn't any feet.

Four other oysters followed them,
    and yet another four;
And thick and fast they came at last,
    And more, and more, and more—
All hopping through the frothy waves
    And scrambling to the shore.

"That was mean!" Alice said indignantly. In the operetta *Alice* by Savile Clarke, Lewis Carroll "mollified oyster sympathizers" by having the Walrus and the Carpenter take a nap and suffer nightmares in which the oyster ghosts sang, danced, and stamped on their chests. If the Walrus and the Carpenter had known Senoi dream techniques, which were allegedly in practice in Malaysia at that time, they could have stopped the ghosts from tormenting them and learned a song and dance from them instead.

Marvel in Malaya

News of the phenomenal tribe called the Senoi (more properly, the Temiar branch of the Senoi) who live deep in the rain forest of the Central Range of the Malay Peninsula, spread across the United States in 1969 when Kilton Stewart's 1950 article "Dream Theory in Malaya" appeared in Dr. Charles T. Tart's anthology *Altered States of Consciousness*.[2] Among people who were interested in dreams this article came like the discovery of the Pepys diary and the planetary model of the atom combined. It was a document of immense historical and anthropologial significance, and it provided a dynamic new model of dream work. Stewart announced that the Senoi tribe has been free of violent crime, armed conflict, stress from cultural change, and most chronic mental and physical ailments for probably two or three centuries. These people have almost unearthly psychological integration and emotional maturity because of the way they work with their dreams. Stewart said that they are as advanced psychologically as we are in physics and technology, and he explained their simple system.

The story of this new Garden of Eden and its truly noble savages and their proven answer to life's problems spread quickly. It was retold by Stanley Krippner in *Psychology Today* in 1970,[3] and then in 1972 it really exploded in print. Theodore Roszak told the story in *Where the Wasteland Ends,*[4] Richard Ornstein told it in *The Psychology of Consciousness,*[5] and Ann Faraday told it in *Dream Power.*[6] These were all highly influential popular books.

A high school textbook published in 1972, *Psychology for You,*[7] gave more of its dream chapter to the Senoi than to Carl Jung and Gestalt Therapy together. Since 1972 the Senoi phenomenon has been mentioned in almost all books and articles that consider the meaning of dreams.

In 1973 Marilyn Ferguson's fascinating book *The Brain Revolution* mistakenly credited Kilton Stewart with studying the Senoi society for fifteen years, observing, "The Senoi have become the objects of such intense interest on the part of anthropologists and psychologists that one wonders if they still have time to dream."[8] Ferguson said that several colleges were offering courses in Senoi-inspired dream therapy, that one group of American students had already lived for a year and a half in a communal society copying that of the Senoi, and that some psychologists were using Senoi techniques in group therapy.

It was in 1972 that California psychology professor Patricia Garfield first heard of the Senoi; and her book *Creative Dreaming,*[9] published in 1974, made the Senoi story better known than ever, with her colorful, detailed descriptions of their idyllic life in the jungle and her simple explanation of how to use their dream techniques to enhance and enrich life in our society. The key to Senoi theory is to learn to turn all dreams to good account while dreaming. Thinking about this and intending to do it help it to happen. This is the heart of Senoi education. By discussing the family's dreams at breakfast every morning, the father or older brother teaches the children to recall and value their dreams and to expect to work wonders in their dreams. (Senoi popularizers have failed to include the fact that dreams of females were not important in Senoi culture.[10])

Garfield says that she got most of her information from the extensive writings of Kilton Stewart, who spent several years observing the tribe. Garfield no doubt meant that Stewart spent several years considering the tribe after spending a few months observing them in 1935. He wrote very little about the Senoi.

There is no indication in any of Stewart's writing that he attempted to learn the Senoi language. The only language that Stewart was interested in was the language of dreams.

As recently as December 1978 sleep researcher Rosalind Dymond Cartwright told the Senoi story again in *Psychology Today*.[11] In this telling Kilton Stewart was an anthropologist who visited the Senoi in the 1950s instead of a psychologist who visited them in the 1930s. Cartwright's version of the story may be one of the last ones.

Very Human Behavior

A shocking claim was published in the June 1978 issue of *Human Behavior* magazine. Two young men, Peter Bloch and David Boatwright, went to see the Senoi to film a documentary about their dream-centered culture. The Senoi reportedly told them that they have no interest in the dreams of ordinary people. Like many tribes, they value only the dreams of their shamans. Block and Boatwright, crestfallen, consulted Cambridge's authority on the Senoi, Richard Benjamin, who reportedly confirmed their discovery that the Senoi do not have even the memory of a dream-centered culture.

Shortly after the publication of this new information I had the chance to ask Senoi popularizer Patricia Garfield her opinion of the matter after a lecture. She had obviously given the matter some thought, and she answered graciously that, even if Kilton Stewart's story turns out to be erroneous, the dream method is excellent.

I discussed the whole matter on the telephone with Kilton Stewart's sister, Ida Stewart Coppolino, a recently retired California professor of education. Coppolino recalls vividly her brother's charismatic personality, his lifelong enthusiasm about dreams, and his zestful talents. She was sixteen years younger than Kilton Stewart, but he returned from his travels often and took a lively interest in all the family. It was quite an event when he came home, because word would spread and people would congregate at the family home to hear his latest adventures. Coppolino says that this extraordinary brother was no writer, no saint, and no scientist, but that he was a highly intuitive and effective New York therapist. She let me borrow her personal copies of her brother's thesis and essays.

Clara Stewart Flagg did not care to comment upon her first husband or his work in any way, but sent me a notice about her next dream workshop in Los Angeles in case I would like to enroll.

I studied literature by and about Kilton Stewart,[12] piecing together his career the best I could. My conclusion is that his visit to the Senoi was four months at the longest and that he obtained most of whatever information he had about Senoi dream culture from H. D. "Pat" Noone, a most unusual Englishman who was murdered by Senoi friends. The Senoi were already suffering from diseases, fear of evil spirits, crop failures, and contact with other cultures when Stewart met them. Later they served in military units after World War II, were displaced because of Malaysian political problems, and were further absorbed into the mixed culture of Malaysia by the time Stewart first wrote about them. His article attracted no attention in his lifetime. Kilton Stewart died in 1965 after surgery for lung cancer, never having attained the academic respectability and fame that he would have enjoyed.

In what appears to be Stewart's last writing about dreams, "You Can Raise Your Dream I.Q.," he refers to the findings of Kleitman, Dement and Aserinski and claims that they corroborate his observations in Malaya in 1935. He says that he recorded brand new songs from sleeping shamans throughout the night in periods that correlate with what we now know to be REM periods. (He does not say how he knew the songs were original or how he recorded them without knowing the language or having any sound recording equipment with him.) In the morning the shamans sang him the new songs they had learned in their dreams and had sung aloud while they were asleep. Stewart seems not to have been aware of the major difficulty in his story: research indicates that people do not talk or sing aloud in REM periods. (They talk aloud in their deepest sleep and cannot remember those materials in the morning.) If Stewart really heard people singing entire original songs in REM sleep, which they reproduced upon awakening, this is extremely important data which will alter current findings about the physiology of sleep.

I corresponded with Charles Tart, who started the whole Senoi tradition in the United States by including Stewart's essay in his book, all in good faith. Tart says that it is difficult for him to comment on the original validity of the anthropological claims in the essay in light of the fact that the cultures of Malaysia did not survive the war intact. He does *not* think that the system will be found in full, living form there today, even if more people go looking for it. Times have changed too much.

Tart points out that the validity of Stewart's dream techniques themselves have to be found in practice not in Malaysia. Many people have reported to him that they have had benefits from these techniques. "Even if Stewart made it all up," he concludes, "the basic idea is correct, and that's what matters."

Just before the fateful news item came out in *Human Behavior,* a Los Angeles counselor led a public dream workshop, which was announced this way:

The Ple-Temiar Senoi are a creative and autonomous Malaysian tribe who have known virtually no violence or insanity for nearly three centuries.

The Senoi consider the "dream universe" as real and valuable as the "waking life." Their arts, literature, music, and even their technology, are based on gifts and symbols originally obtained from "spirits" in the dream universe.

The Senoi recognize the "spirits" as images of their own personality. The goal of their dreamwork—done in family or community groups—is to befriend their dream spirits, to make spirits into allies which provide support in waking life as well.

Six months later the same counselor led another workshop in the same place and changed the announcement this way:

Dreams are creative expressions of our selves. Neither Senoi nor Gestalt dreamwork attempts to "analyze" or "interpret" dreams; instead, both encourage the dreamer to experience his or her dream directly, and to discover whatever unique message it may hold.

GESTALT THERAPY provides techniques which allow the individual to integrate the various parts of the dream. In doing so, the dreamer experiences a new sense of wholeness.

SENOI DREAMWORK is based on the culture of a Malaysian tribe. The goal of all Senoi dreamwork is to befriend dream "spirits," to use them as allies who provide support in the "dream universe" or in the "waking life."

Six months later she led another dream workshop and did not mention the Senoi in her announcement at all.

It looks as if that large shift of emphasis is going to occur across the country. Stewart's essay was read as scientific language for most of a decade; in the future it may be read as poetical language. C. S. Lewis said that the difference between scientific language and poetical language is emphatically not that the first utters truth and the second fancies. Everything that is real is a real something, although it is not necessarily what it pretends to be. "What pretends to be a crocodile may be a (real) dream; what pretends at the breakfast-table to be a dream may be a (real) lie."[13]

Notes

1. James Sutherland, ed., *Oxford Book of Literary Anecdotes* (New York: Simon and Schuster, 1975), p. 213.
2. Charles Tart, *Altered States of Consciousness* (Garden City, New York: Doubleday, 1969).
3. Stanley Krippner and William Hughes, "Sleep, Unease and Dreams," *Psychology Today,* (June 1970), 40–41.
4. Theodore Roszak, *Where the Wasteland Ends* (Garden City, New York: Doubleday, 1973).
5. Richard Ornstein, *The Psychology of Consciousness* (New York: Viking Press, 1972).
6. Ann Faraday, *Dream Power* (New York: Coward, McCann & Geoghegan, Inc., 1972).
7. Sol Gordon, *Psychology for You* (New York: Oxford Book Co., 1972).
8. Marilyn Ferguson, *The Brain Revolution* (New York: Bantam Books, 1975), p. 163.
9. Patricia Garfield, *Creative Dreaming* (New York: Ballantine Books, 1974).
10. Kilton Riggs Stewart, *Religious Beliefs and Practises* (sic.) *in Primitive Society— A Sociological Interpretation of Their Therapeutic Aspects,* p. 114.

11. Rosalind Dymond Cartwright, "Happy Endings for Our Dreams," *Psychology Today,* (December 1978), 66–76.

12. I studied the following materials:

a. Kilton Riggs Stewart, *Religious Beliefs and Practises* (sic) *in Primitive Society —A Sociological Interpretation of Their Therapeutic Aspects,* an unpublished thesis submitted to London School of Economics and Political Science in 1947. This thesis should be carefully examined by anyone trying to ascertain the rigorousness of Stewart's scholarship.

b. Kilton Stewart, *Pygmies and Dream Giants* (New York: Harper & Row, 1954). This book gives insight into Stewart's background and values; it does not mention the Senoi.

c. Kilton Stewart, *Creative Psychology and Dream Education.* This private publication of Stewart's has no date on it, but it was printed circa 1960. It includes:

(1) "Introduction"

(2) "Education and the Split Personality" reprinted from *Mental Hygiene,* July 1943.

(3) "The Mental Age of the Sleep Mind"

(4) "Dream Theory in Malaya" reprinted from *Complex,* 1951.

(5) "You Can Raise Your Dream I.Q."

d. Richard Noone with Dennis Holman, *In Search of the Dream People* (New York: William Morrow and Company, 1972). Data in this book conflicts with some of Stewart's claims.

13. C. S. Lewis, *The Personal Heresy (London: Oxford University Press, 1939), p. 109.*

EIGHT

THE TIME OF OUR LIVES: TRUE PERCEPTIONS

"It's a poor kind of memory that only works backwards," the Queen remarked.

Lewis Carroll, *Through the Looking Glass*

Getting the Message

Lewis Carroll told about a man who worked so hard at believing so much one day that, when he was told it was raining outside, he didn't have any ability left to believe one more thing; and so he went out without his umbrella and got drenched. That story was not true, which adds to Carroll's irony. If people think the things in this chapter are lies, that is understandable. There is a limit to how much we can believe at once.

I did not originally intend to share the following material, which is mostly about how dreams are not bound by time. A dream made me change my mind. This material is essential to the subject.

I dreamed that I saw an unopened envelope on my desk from someone named Fanny Graft. That's all. It was hypnagogic imagery that came as I slipped back to sleep while considering a morning REM dream in which I was exploring the many rooms of a house of dreams. "A dream not understood is like a letter not opened." I knew that old saying from the Talmud. But this unopened dream letter seemed ridiculous. I was getting to know my dreams well enough to be fairly sure that it was at least a joke, not utter nonsense. I would try to "open the envelope." First I had to see what "Fanny Graft" meant.

I never heard the name Fanny Graft before. The only Fanny I ever knew was my algebra teacher, Fanny Steel. Are Steel and Graft connected? Only in that graft and steal are words to do with thievery. I was sure this Fanny was Fanny Steel. What does thievery mean to me? "Procrastination is the thief of time" came to mind before anything else.

I started to get the message. It's been about thirty years since Fanny Steel played an extremely strange role in my life. The envelope dream was telling me that I had a letter thirty years old still unopened. I had a dream not understood. I didn't tell anyone about that dream at the time I had it, and I have told very few people since, because I don't like people to think that I am deluded.

One morning I awakened from a very vivid, disturbing dream and went over it in detail in my mind. I had walked into my algebra classroom in Willard Junior High School in Santa Ana as usual, but I was struck by the unusual quality of light that met my eyes. The sun was hitting the classroom windows in a beautiful new way. It must have been brilliant fall sunlight on a day with Santana wind. Miss Steel was at the windows adjusting the old dark green shades, cutting out the glare the best she could and watching us enter. When class began, she revealed a surprise test on the blackboard before me. I was shocked. As we took the test, she made me move from my seat at the front to the back of the room.

The reason I have often thought about that dream and rarely

spoken of it is that when I actually went to my real class that day the unusual quality of light was there and Miss Steel was trying to adjust the old green shades while watching us enter. It was the unique scene in my dream exactly. I was sure we wouldn't have a surprise test, because Miss Steel had told us all about the course and had never mentioned any possible surprise tests. Besides, that would be too much of a coincidence.

She gave us the surprise test on the board.

I finished the test and sat mulling this over in my mind, jubilant that I hadn't had to leave my seat. I wanted to prove that the dream was at least partly wrong. There was no room in my antireligious home or my fundamentalist church for dreams coming true today. I would be blamed in either place if I told about this ridiculous experience.

"Kay," Miss Steel said, "Steve can't see the board well. Let him have your seat here at the front, and you sit at the back in his desk the rest of the period."

I objected very strongly and silently as I moved to the back. Why did this have to happen to me? It undid everything. Now I would never again be able to believe in my heart that time works as simply as we have been told. It seemed a bit like the times when I played old records on a wind-up Victrola with a worn-out fiber needle, and I could hear the words that were still to come softly in the background of the present words of the song. All the song, from beginning to end, was on the record. But we only expect to hear one word at a time because we don't expect the needle to pick up more than that. Could I be like a needle picking up vibrations from two grooves at once as I moved along the record of my life? It was a perplexing idea.

The sun never hit the window quite that way again. Miss Steel never stood at the shades that way either. We never had another surprise test. I never had to trade seats there again. And I didn't have any more dreams like that for several years. But my view of reality was never quite the same after that strange, bright morning. I have taken dreams fairly seriously ever since.

The envelope dream caused me to evaluate how greatly the test dream has influenced me, but it also suggested that the test dream was symbolic. As I reflect upon Fanny Steel, I remember my frustration the first week or two in her class. I went in after school one day, probably trembling, and told her that, with her permission, I would have to drop out of the class because I couldn't understand what she was talking about. Her eyes twinkled a bit behind her glasses as she very confidently assured me, in her relaxed way, that if I would be patient I would soon find it all clear and easy. She seemed so wise and kind that I half believed her.

I was distressed in this bizarre, esoteric world of illogic where X is suddenly taken out of ox and axe and made to pose as anything from 1500 to $(Y + Z)$. Miss Steel was right, and before another week passed I had caught on and fallen in love with algebra. Perhaps I fell in love with the idea of symbols also.

Fanny and Mary Jane Steel were two unmarried sisters who lived together and taught together all their lives. Mary Jane was sharp, crisp, and focused. She taught me American government. She was all facts and intellect. Fanny was larger, softer, less focused; she taught me algebra. She was all processes and understanding. They were two of the best teachers I had met, and yet they had such different styles that I thought of them as two sides of a coin. Now I think of them as representing my rational faculty and my intuitive faculty.

To me Fanny Steel herself is a symbol of our faculty for understanding dreams. She tells us it will become clear and easy if we are patient. Without being presumptuous about the value of this book, I suspect that the light and the surprise test refer to this writing.

More than two years before the envelope from Fanny Graft appeared on my dream desk, I had a dream with the word *Fanny* in it that I did not understand at all. Mr. and Mrs. Owen Barfield were visiting me in my childhood home, and we went out to the back alley where I used to play and where many of my dreams have taken place. Suddenly we were in the heart of London in front of the Athaeneum Club, with its Greek architectural style, and a new ultra-modern building that stood next to it. I asked Mrs. Barfield if I should study for a degree in history and, if so, what kind of employment I should seek. She urged me to earn a degree in history and then to get a job mowing lawns, because pushing a lawnmower does wonders for the fanny. (I have never met Mrs. Barfield in real life; and I am not fat, as she seemed to imply.) I jotted the dream down and left it gladly.

Knowing who Fanny was now, I went back to that dream. It occurred to me that, although mowing lawns means cutting grass to my thinking self, it means pushing forward to my body. Mrs. Barfield was urging me to study my personal dream history from childhood onward and to push forward in my understanding of dream symbols. I failed to take her good advice at the time because I didn't know what she was talking about. Once I had the meaning of the key word *fanny*, the whole thing opened up easily. Obviously, dreams with personal symbols in them can't open up easily to anyone except the dreamer. People who keep dream records say that later dreams can explain earlier dreams. I agree.

Looking Ahead

One of the few people who heard the original Fanny Steel dream story was my husband. I was frustrated that he didn't trust my judgment enough to think it could be true. There is an ideal way to convince people, and it requires very good luck. In 1960 we were on an educational tour of Europe and Russia. One day we were walking on a path at Villa d'Este outside Rome, a hillside garden covered with ingenious fountains. The whole place was alive with the sound of splashing water. We had never heard of it before we joined this tour and hadn't known what to expect ahead of time.

As we wandered along, I suddenly grabbed John's arm and stopped him. "This spot is just like a place I dreamed about months ago," I exclaimed. "In my dream we went around the bend ahead, beyond that clump of trees, and there was a large shady pool. On the far side of the dark pool there was a waterfall dropping into it, and behind the waterfall people were walking back and forth behind the water."

"How could people walk behind a waterfall?" he answered absently, not much impressed by such a trivial memory. We walked around the bend, and there, without warning, was a large dark pool before us. On the far side there was a waterfall with people walking back and forth behind it. This time John stopped of his own accord. His face blanched. It was the exact scene I had just described. He is an honest man, and I am an honest woman, and this was too much evidence for him to brush aside. That is when he began to gradually and carefully modify his view of dreams and time.

I have never cared about convincing any other people of these facts. I think that precognition in dreams is a relatively common and unimportant fact of life. I learned just recently that my son Peter has precognitive dreams occasionally and has never bothered to mention them because he assumed that it was one more of life's little mysteries that everyone takes for granted. He figured that it is just in the nature of dreams to peek ahead. He is only ten, and I think he is absolutely right.

John Calvin took precognitive dreams for granted also, but he considered them evidence of human immortality. "Indeed, sleep itself, which benumbs man, seeming to deprive him of life, is no obscure witness of immortality, since it suggests not only thoughts of things that have never happened, but also presentiments of the future."[1]

If the following examples of my many precognitive dreams do not seem especially interesting, they illustrate the point that many precognitive dreams are not very interesting. In college once I dreamed of some vivid colored scenes; less than twenty-four hours later I was unexpectedly taken to see the new movie *Picnic*. I had not seen previews or advertising for it, but the very scenes in my dream appeared in the movie. At about the same time I dreamed once that I rode in a car in which the knob was missing off the stick for the gear shift. The following day I got rides with completely unrelated, unacquainted people in two different cars with gear-shift knobs missing. I never saw another car like that before or since.

In August 1975 I dreamed I was visiting the home of someone's sister named Christie Ann, and she was the daughter of a quiet woman who stayed in the background. A little over two weeks later I met Lucille Sider Dayton at a conference in Chicago. She invited me, along with some other Christian feminists, to her home on Christiana Street, which served as the editorial office of *Daughters of Sarah* magazine. I did not realize this coincidence until I read my dream again later. I've never met a Christie Ann. In January 1979 I happened to tell this dream to someone (other than my husband) for the first time. It was Walden Howard, editor of *Faith at Work* magazine. He said, "That's funny. My daughter is named Christie Ann.'

One June morning I dreamed I went into a store where I shop and saw old Easter baskets on sale. I met an extremely friendly man by the baskets. The next day when I went to my grocery store, they had actually put out some old Easter baskets for sale; I have never seen that done out of season before or since. That day I met an unusually responsive and sensitive man who became a permanent friend.

One night as I was drifting off to sleep I was awakened by the words "Body charities!" I wrote it down. The next morning at 9 A.M. I was awakened by a call from the Red Cross asking for my husband to donate blood. They had never called before, and I didn't know they had his name.

Several of my morning precognitive dreams have been about what was on my front porch for me. In August 1978 I dreamed that I had my hair in a long, thick braid that I was admiring, thinking that it was the latest style. After I got up, I flipped through an Avon catalog that had been left on my porch. There was the very braid I had dreamed I was wearing, on a stylish model. On her it looked good. A few months later I dreamed I was looking right into the face of a dark haired orchestra conductor. I got up and took the mail out of my box and found myself looking into the face of Zubin Mehta on the cover of *Newsweek*.

My favorite of all my front porch dreams is the one in which my old friend Beverly appeared at a church beach party, although she does not go to my church and does not like the beach. During our devotions Beverly started to gesture for me to leave my group and come to her to talk. I headed toward her in the dream and then was abruptly awakened by someone knocking on my front door. I went to the door and peeked out, and there was Beverly, whom I had not seen for over a year. She said she had been ringing the doorbell and knocking for five minutes or more. She was beginning to think I might not be home. Although she does not like to drive, she had come many miles to see me without even calling first, because she wanted to take me out for breakfast and tell me in person about the fact that she was suddenly in love and engaged to be married.

Twice in dreams I got important news about friends without their having told me. I dreamed that our neighbors were buying a new house and moving away from us. I had a compulsion to tell my neighbor the dream, foolish as I felt about it. She answered that the idea had never crossed her mind, but later I learned that she was already in the process of buying her new house when I had the dream and told her about it; they soon moved. Later I dreamed that my friend Thora told me she was expecting a baby. Once again I could get no peace until I told my dream. I felt silly about it, partly because Thora already had four children. She answered sincerely that if she were expecting, it was news to her. Thora's son Thomas was born almost nine months after the dream.

I seem to check up on my husband even in my sleep. One morning early in 1965 I dreamed he opened a can and the label came off. When I got up after he left for work, I found that very can in the refrigerator. Once when John was gone to a university class on dreaming, I took a nap and dreamed that I got a test back, and to my dismay I got a C when I had expected an A. I didn't know that John had taken a test that had not yet been returned. He got it back at about the time I was dreaming about my test score, and to his surprise he received a C when he had expected an A. (It had been scored wrong.)

Another morning I dreamed that I discovered John and another man ready to crush grapes in a large container, and to my dismay John was about to step in with his shoes on. I tried to stop him, but he insisted that the directions required him to crush the grapes with his shoes on. Later that day John felt a strong urge to tell me a silly story he had heard Paul Harvey tell on the radio that morning, although I can't stand Paul Harvey. The story was that there was a kind of health-food wine made from grapes that are crushed by peasants wearing orthopedic shoes. I groaned.

Twice I have seemed to spy upon people who weren't that close to me. The first time I dreamed that in my Bethel teacher training class I declared as a joke "I am a genius!" and everyone laughed.

I had a feeling that was pleasant but strangely unfamiliar to me. The dream came true, but it was my friend Shiela who said the words in class the night after my dream. Watching her face closely, I knew exactly how she felt, from the inside, during the laughter. I had felt her feeling in advance.

In my other memorable snooping dream, I found myself in bed with a large young black man, making love very passionately. (My husband is not large, young, or black, and I had never before had explicit, illicit sexual adventures in my dreams that I know of.) I felt a quality of utter reality in this dream, and after I awoke I believed it was factual rather than my invention. A few hours later I was with a woman whose name is almost the same as mine. She informed me that her new lover was a large young black man and that I would never know how good sex could be unless I did it that way. I don't have the vaguest idea what I answered. I'm grateful that one Kinsey Report dream was the extent of my survey; I have no desire to experience other people's private lives.

When I was a child I experienced the overwhelming emotion of just having given birth.[2] I have been denied the privilege of giving birth in my life, but because of the dream I know the appropriate emotion as well as many women who have had the experience. This seems to me to be slightly related to the dream that a wise professor friend of mine recalls vividly. He dreamed that he was pregnant just before his wife gave birth to their only child thirty years ago. The feeling in that dream is still important to him.

In 1968 I confided in Dr. Richard H. Bube of Stanford University and the American Scientific Affiliation about a few of my experiences, knowing that he was not well disposed toward extrasensory perception. One story I told him was of the morning when I dreamed that my young son Jonathan came into the bedroom with his irreplaceable rabbit balloon that he prized and asked his father to blow it up bigger. I watched while John blew it up extra large and popped it. I awoke and watched with dismay while Jonathan walked right in with that balloon and asked his father to blow it up. I watched in distress while John blew it up bigger than ever. I was torn about what to do. The balloon popped and Jonathan was unconsolable.

Dr. Bube wrote back with the same question I had worried

about. "Suppose that because of your dream of the popping of your son's cherished balloon, you had stopped your husband from blowing it up. Would the balloon have had to pop some way anyway in order to fulfill the predictive dream? Or, if the predictive dream could have been used to prevent the occurrence of the event predicted, from what source could the warning of an event *not to occur* have come?" I did not learn until years later that P. D. Ouspensky's theory of spiral time[3] would fully and perfectly explain those questions for anyone who believes in spiral time, a development of Pythagorus' theory of eternal recurrence. This theory is well illustrated in the pleasant play by J. B. Priestly *I Have Been Here Before,* which dramatizes the idea that we live our lives over and over with the chance of improving them. "Foreseeing" is recall! If we don't accept spiral time, we have to live with some logical and linguistic difficulties until a better theory comes along to answer Dr. Bube's question, so far as I can see.

In the meantime, I think the best response to Bube's (and my) question is the illogical response given by Lewis Carroll:

"What sort of things do you remember best?" Alice ventured to ask.
"Oh, things that happened the week after next," the Queen replied in a careless tone. "For instance, now," she went on ... "there's the King's Messenger. He's in prison now, being punished: and the trial doesn't even begin till next Wednesday: and of course the crime comes last of all."
"Suppose he never commits the crime?" said Alice.
" That would be all the better, wouldn't it?" the Queen said.
Through the Looking-Glass

Intimations of Mortality

The kind of precognitive dream that has interested most people through history, apparently, is the dream that reveals bodily conditions. Hippocrates, the father of medicine, believed in such dreams. In some cultures dreams are believed to diagnose ailments, in some they predict ailments, and in some they are believed to prescribe medical treatment or to help directly. The Navajos, for example, look to dreams only for diagnosis.

Once I had a very vivid dream of a dog biting my right thumb and refusing to let go, no matter what. Within a few days I developed a joint pain in my thumb base where his teeth had been, and it has never gone away. It bothers me when I carry heavy objects or try to open jar lids.

Once when I was seriously ill I dreamed that my friend Anne Wakefield, who is a fine artist and weaver, was unhappy because her knitting was raveled. People told me that she knit very poorly, and I could see how loose and irregular her work was, with stitches missing. That is a joke to anyone who knows Anne. But Ann is my middle name. *Raveled* always reminds me of Shakespeare's line in *Macbeth,* "Sleep that knits up the ravell'd sleeve of care...." *Wake* from the name *Wakefield,* meant that I wasn't getting adequate sleep, although I was in bed full time, to knit up the damage that was taking place. I didn't understand the dream at the time.

What really surprised me was looking at the dreams surrounding my emergency appendectomy in the spring of 1978. Six days before the surgery I dreamed that a comet was coming near the earth soon and that when it arrived we would go into a kind of laboratory to try to counteract the damage it does to our bodies. I did not know that anything was wrong with me. The same night I dreamed that Elizabeth Skoglund died. Skoglund is another southern California author whose name is sometimes confused with mine. Three days before surgery I dreamed I was at a long meeting and had a foul-smelling toilet along with me. Two days before surgery I dreamed I was sharing a tiny apartment with an old friend who in reality lives in an expensive home at the beach. There was a metal rod placed so low that if we hung our dresses on it they would drag on the floor. A fat little lady came in and lingered, and I wanted very much for her to leave. (In two days I would share a hospital room with a lady who lives in an expensive home at the beach. The bed rail looked like the metal rod too low for hanging dresses. A fat little nurse bothered me a lot, and I wanted her to leave the room.) On the night before I learned I had appendicitis and was rushed into surgery, I dreamed I had a small but intensely infected sore on my face. Three days after the appendectomy I dreamed that I had lost a tiny red purse! The connection of all these dreams is obvious now; they meant nothing to me at the time.

One night in 1974 I dreamed that I was in a really terrible earthquake. The world was roaring apart outside, and my building was going to collapse and crush me. This was the end. Unaware of my dream, my husband John dreamed the very next night that he saw collisions among the stars in the sky and that this cataclysm in space was probably going to consume the earth. On the third night I dreamed that a wild tiger was rushing about in a yard to kill people and that I stood at a door to keep him out and to let people into the house if they could get past him. I didn't know where John was and felt the tiger was going to slay him. It happened that my father, like my husband, was named John. A few hours after this third dream my father died in his front yard of a heart attack, while trying to get to the house. We had no more dreams of earthshaking cataclysms until my appendicitis in 1978.

I suspect that this is the stuff that superstitions can build from. If we dream about cataclysms in space again, I won't make any assumptions at all, but I will probably pray for extra protection and guidance. If another dream dog bites me, I will do the same.

I have only had one dream that prescribed a cure for a disease, and it is not a disease I have ever had. On April 19, 1978, I learned in my sleep "A natural part of the pumpkin seed, *yavis,* will cure alcoholism." Three days later, on April 22, I read in my copy of *Human Behavior* which arrived that day that a chemical called THP can produce alcoholism and that neuropsychologists at Purdue University wished to produce a corresponding drug that could reduce or cure alcoholism. I don't know if the news in my dream that burned in my mind and awakened me was mere wish fulfillment in response to the future article or a true revelation from God. I wish the Purdue neuropsychologists would try pumpkin seed extracts first of all. If *yavis* works, I'll share the Nobel Prize in medicine with them.

It was well after these various physical health dreams of mine that I read about the great physician who used the name Philippus Paracelsus (1493–1541). Paracelsus lived in Zurich at the same time as Calvin's colleague Heinrich Bullinger. Robert Browning wrote *Paracelsus* as a tribute to this controversial genius, and Zurich's later sage Carl Jung read and admired him. I have a hunch that Paracelsus was a figure in my complex Swiss pageant dream about Calvin and Jung.

Paracelsus said this about dreams: "That which the dream shows is the shadow of such wisdom as exists in the man, even if during his waking state he may know nothing about it, for we ought to know that God has given us our own wisdom and knowledge, reason, and the power to perceive the past and the future; but we do not know it, because we are fooling away our time with outward and perishing things, and are asleep in regard to that which is real within ourself."[4]

Time and Eternity

The idea that time is relative came to Albert Einstein early one morning just as he got out of bed. This was the knowledge that the events which are simultaneous for one observer are not necessarily simultaneous for another.[5] Einstein's well known remark on the subject is hard to accept but quite undeniable: "For us believing physicists, this separation between past, present and future has the value of mere illusion, however tenacious."[6]

People who are naturally offended by such talk might as well acknowledge their honest distaste for the relativity of time without assuming that it is an un-Christian idea. When the Bible states that God is the same yesterday, today, and forever, it is at heart pointing us beyond time as we know it. When the Bible says that a thousand years is as one day to God and one day is as a thousand years, that is relativity pre-Einstein.

Arthur Koestler has written that to the visual thinker time loses the awesome, cast-iron character it automatically assumes in verbal thought. Einstein did much of his brilliant thinking in images rather than logical sentences. Some people speculate now that there are two kinds of time: our usual movement through past, present, and future; and another kind of time that includes it all at once and is the domain of physics, religion, dreams and precognition.

This sounds rather like C. S. Lewis' distinction between time and eternity. Lewis explained in *The Discarded Image* that eternity is quite distinct from perpetuity, from mere endless continuance in time. Eternity is not, like perpetuity, an endless series of moments, each lost as soon as it is attained. Eternity is timeless, a plenitude of unlimited life that no amount of time can equal. Time, no matter how endless, is hopelessly transitory. If an infinite amount of time is the best image that we can get of eternity, it is still almost a parody of eternity. God, Lewis insists, is eternal not perpetual. "He never *fore*sees; He simply sees. Your 'future' is only an area, and only for us a special area, of His infinite Now."[7]

C. S. Lewis once began a horror story about time travel to another world that was making a very evil copy of our world. (This fragment is now published in a collection called *The Dark Tower*.[8]) In it Lewis refers to the theory of J. W. Dunne, a mathematician and engineer who published *An Experiment with Time* in 1927.[9] Dunne's theory of serial time has fascinated many people, including his friend J. B. Priestly, who wrote an excellent play about it called *Time and the Conways*. Christian author J. Stafford Wright claimed in his book *Man in the Process of Time*, "Since reading Dunne's book I have often noticed precognitive elements in my own dreams."[10]

From a completely objective observation of his own dream life and dreams of people he knew Dunne gathered that our dreams reflect future events just about as often as past events. He wanted to know why time is "mixed" in that we often have first the dream, then the memory of the dream, then the experience that prompted the dream, and finally the memory of the experience.

Basically, Dunne felt forced to propose that, as one aspect of a person lives in the fourth dimension, moving along in time, another aspect of that person observes his or her entire life pattern at once from the fifth, the eternal, dimension. Dreams, he observed, come from the fifth dimension. To his great surprise Dunne developed the first scientific argument for human immortality.

Dunne worked out an involved plan for technical experimentation and urged future researchers to complete his statistics on precognitive dreams and to recast physics and psychology according to serialism for a sounder approach to truth. Fifty years later it seems that no one has responded to the challenge yet. C. P. Snow has claimed that scientists take great pride in knowing what subjects not to think about.

At least three thousand years before Dunne started recording his dreams every morning and getting friends to do the same, the Hindu *Vedas* advised us that morning dreams are more apt to come true, and writers ever since have been telling us that news, from Homer and Horace and Ovid down to the Bible expositor Alexander Maclaren in our own century.

Famous Prophetic Dreams

Unfortunately, stories like that of St. Odilia give prophetic dreams a bad name. Odilia was born blind in 660 and received her sight when she was baptized as a girl. She is a popular saint in Germany and France. In the two world wars her purported account of dreaming about these wars became popular, but authorities claim that she did not write the account at all.

Another popular prophetic dreamer has been John Chapman, a fifteenth-century tinker in Swaffam, England. He had three dreams that told him to journey to London and meet on London Bridge a man who would make him rich. He obeyed and met a man who asked what he was doing on the bridge. He answered that a dream had sent him there. The man remarked that a recent dream had instructed him to journey to Swaffam and dig up a jar of gold coins that rested under the only tree of a tinker named John Chapman. Chapman kept quiet, went home, and became a rich man. His memorial is in the Swaffam church, to which he contributed generously. The story sounds too good to be true.

There is better evidence for the remarkable aid that once came to Sir E. W. Budge in a dream. He had a triple dream on the night before his fateful examination on ancient Oriental languages, between midnight and 2 A.M., showing him just what the test would be. He got up and studied the obscure material from 2 A.M. until time for the examination. His dream had been accurate in every detail, and he won the fellowship that made possible his career as keeper of Egyptian antiquities at the British Museum.

A few weeks before the accidental death of Mark Twain's

brother, Twain reportedly dreamed he saw the young man in a coffin in a detailed setting. It all came about exactly as it was in the dream. Twain was quick to debunk all foolish superstition, but he always felt he contributed to his brother's tragic death. He had recommended heroics to his brother after the warning dream.

Charles Dickens was a fussy sleeper and a heavy dreamer. He insisted that his head must point north at night, and he slept in the exact center of a very smooth bed. (He mentioned dreams about twenty times in *David Copperfield* and described the agony of tossing in a rumpled bed.) One Thursday night he dreamed vividly of a lady in a red shawl who said she was Miss Napier. He thought it was silly for such an empty dream to be so vivid. Friday evening he met Miss Napier, red shawl and all. Nothing more came of the incident.

Two of the most touching accounts of precognitive dreaming relate to famous disasters. In 1966 a half million tons of coal slag buried part of the village of Aberfan, Wales, and killed well over a hundred children in their schools. Reporters afterward learned that many of the victims and other people had dreamed beforehand of masses of black coming down on them. The other account is Ward Hill Lamon's description of how his friend Abraham Lincoln was oppressed in his last two weeks by a dream that had foretold his assassination. When Lincoln next looked into his Bible he turned by chance to Jacob's dream and then discovered how much emphasis the entire Bible puts on dreams and visions. He remarked that in his day dreams were regarded as very foolish but that if we believe the Bible we must accept the fact that in the old days God used dreams. Lincoln shared that observation shortly before he died, hoping that his dream was not true.

John Newton had died two years before Lincoln was born, but he too played a role in the abolition of slavery. After working in the slave trade as a ship captain, he was converted and eventually became a minister and hymn writer in England. Three of his hymns still sung today are "Amazing Grace," "How Sweet the Name of Jesus Sounds," and "Glorious Things of Thee Are Spoken." Newton said of dreams, "Those who acknowledge Scripture will allow that there have been monitory and supernatural dreams, evident communications from heaven, either directing or foretelling future events; and those who are acquainted with the history and experience of the people of God, are well assured that such intimations have not been totally withheld in any period down to the present... '[11] Newton had himself once dreamed an overwhelming symbolic dream that left him disoriented for two or three days. He later forgot it for a few years. When he became a Christian, he saw clearly that his dreams had foretold his conversion.

Research in Redlands

Although I have a special interest in precognitive dreams, my own interesting dream research touched upon other aspects of time instead. When Kleitman and Dement were beginning to revolutionize dream knowledge with their research at Chicago University, I was failing to revolutionize dream knowledge with my research at the University of Redlands in California. As two eighteen-year-old freshmen, my college roommate and I had no idea that current knowledge about dreams was utterly primitive, that the next twenty-five years would bring an absolute boom in dream research, and that what we were doing was worthy of professional attention.

Kathy Crosby is an excellent normal sleeper, and she often took naps when I was studying and usually went to bed for the night while I was studying. One of our main differences was our attitudes about time. I took a heavy academic load and was always short on sleep and always a few minutes late wherever I went. Kathy, in contrast, placed a very high value on getting adequate rest and getting everywhere promptly or early. Another major difference between us was that my own deep interest in dreams was matched by her unusual dream abilities, and my own ordinary dream abilities were matched by her ordinary level of interest in dreams. We were a perfect match; my roommate could converse during her dreams.

Our dream experimentation began one night when Kathy gasped "Oh!" and I said impishly "What's wrong?" She propped herself up in bed, sound asleep, and explained to me in great indignation and grief that a walrus had just bit her knee. This always brings to my mind Melville's vivid imagery, "The Nantucketer, out of sight of land, furls his sails and lays him to his rest, while under his very pillow rush herds of walruses and whales."[12] I was highly amused by Kathy's rude walrus, but I didn't guess that, like Melville's Nantucketer, I was launched on a voyage.   •

I noticed that Kathy had to be asleep a fair amount of time, but not too long, to get into her talkative mood in her sleep. I could sense her readiness to talk by the sleep style her body expressed. In retrospect, I think this usually occurred twenty to sixty minutes after she went to sleep, and I am sure that I would have noticed if there had been eye movement under her lids during those periods. I had observed REM occasionally since childhood. My opinion is that it was in stage four, or bedroom sleep, that Kathy began to open up her dream life to me. She never had the slightest memory of these dreams she communicated to me, no matter when she awakened. Yet she recalled dreams very frequently.

The first, and perhaps the most important, feature that I noted about Kathy's dreaming conversations with me was that, no matter what time of day or night it was, she could always tell me exactly what time it was according to her watch. Many times I asked her to tell me the time and she cheerfully or wearily lifted her arm out in front of her face at the appropriate angle and told me the time to the minute. Her eyes were closed, her arm was bare, and I was at her dresser across the room checking her watch where she kept it when she was in bed. To this day Kathy always knows the time within two minutes and often perfectly whenever she awakens.

One night when Kathy was in a typically playful dream mood she interrupted our conversation by shushing me, turning over, and propping herself up on her elbows. She was obviously listening to the tick of the little alarm clock that she kept on a ledge above her headboard as she inched forward sneakily and poised herself for attack. Suddenly her hand shot out, and she swooped the little clock down and clutched it to her breast. "Got it!" she gloated. Then her face looked conscience-stricken and worried. She lifted the little clock to her ear and listened carefully. "It's still alive," she said with relief, and stroked it tenderly. Her pantomine was so skillful that her clock still seems half-bird in my memory. My guess is that she was acting out a pun because "time flies"; but it was her dream not mine.

Another time Kathy was dreaming that she and her current boyfriend were walking in downtown Redlands together, and she described the scene to me. Then she said she didn't want me following along with them any longer. She never visualized me in these dreams that I knew of but knew me as a familiar consciousness that sometimes accompanied her; we talked about that once in her sleep. This time I asked her to do me the favor of telling me the time before I left her. Feeling uncooperative, she informed me that she had left her watch back in the room on the dresser and did not know the time. I could see her watch on the dresser and thought that was a good joke she played on me, but I suspected that she knew the time anyway. I replied that I had a great need to know the time and that all she had to do was to look in the window of the store she was passing and read the time for me that was on the clock there. She probably told me to read the clock for myself, but she seemed interested and looked at the clock and reported to me the exact time that her watch said in real life. I kept my promise and immediately left her alone with her boyfriend.

I see in a contemporary dream anthology that some soldiers claimed in 1758 that they could influence the dreams of one of their friends by whispering to him in his sleep. Their claim was written out by someone in 1830, and now it is being published in the 1970s as the only example I have found in print of this kind of experiment.[13]

Another time when I looked in on Kathy in a romantic situation she was at a soda fountain having a treat. She giggled and confided to me that the two young men sitting on either side of her, who were indeed friends she liked, were both holding her hand part of the time under the counter and flirting with her, and neither knew what the other was doing it. (Neither knew that I was there, either.) She felt like quite a *femme fatale* encouraging both of them at once. Although the action continued in her dreams when she talked with me, she never had to whisper to keep her dream characters from hearing our conversation. Furthermore, I did not overhear what she said to them. Time passed at its usual rate in her dreams when I was listening in.

Apparently being willingly engaged in conversation with me could keep Kathy in the deep-sleep state for prolonged periods. According to my scribbled notes she went on chatting with me for at least two hours a couple of times. At other times she would just go into a different sleep stage and leave me alone. She would either tell me she was through or lapse into silence.

Kathy sometimes knew that she was dreaming during our conversations, although I don't know what her dreaming concept of the dream experience was. She could probably have given at least as good a description of dreaming while she was dreaming as that most of us can give of waking while we are waking.

It was on October 7, 1953, that I first tried having Kathy drink water in her sleep. She found it no problem at all. At various times she ate raisins, cookies, a sugar lump, and an orange in her sleep. As I recall, she peeled the orange herself. As she recalls, from what I told her the next morning, she expressed concern about cavities, and I suggested that she brush her teeth after eating at night. Accordingly, she would get up after a snack and go across the room with her eyes shut (as they always were), brush her teeth, and return to bed—all sound asleep. Although she could perform all these movements with skill, she never showed any evidence of a tendency toward sleepwalking except when we were conversing and my presence stimulated it.

These events seemed so peculiar to me that I told a couple of our friends about Kathy's sleep talents, and they couldn't believe me at all. The next time Kathy was in an especially active dream mood I slipped out of our room and called three or four friends to sneak in and witness. Kathy could detect the very slight rustle of people tiptoeing into the room and demanded to know who was entering. I told her I had brought her some friends. She declared that she could recognize anyone's voice if that person said the word *four*. Our friend Dawn was fascinated and said *four* in an unnatural voice; Kathy knew immediately that this was Dawn. We told her who was present, and she agreeably demonstrated her time-telling and eating and walking skills for the amazed girls.

Because Kathy awakened vastly better than I did, she usually got me up in the morning. One night I told the dreaming Kathy that I would like her to awaken me the next morning by simply saying "Psalm Thirty," a phrase that I chose out of the blue as the idea came into my mind. The next morning Kathy promptly awakened me by saying "Psalm Thirty" with conviction, as if it were a regular reveille. I made sure that she had no memory of my request and did not know why she had awakened me that way, and then I explained it to her. We both knew that this was like posthypnotic suggestion.

Although Kathy didn't write verse in her waking life that I knew of, she made up spontaneous verses in her sleep while talking to me if she felt like it.

Kathy's sleeping personality was much like her waking personality, but there was much more childlike playfulness and spontaneity in sleep. Something I could not define was missing along with her waking consciousness. I guess now that what I missed most was the "Why?" of her waking mind. She retained many of her interests and knew her preferences in her sleep, but she did not question the peculiar structure of things in that state. She was free to agree or disagree with me, but she never examined the mystery of what was going on when I came into her dreams. Along with this childlike acceptance of what is, free from analysis, I suspect that there was an absence of some of the constraints and defences that are built up in the process of maturation. Kathy seemed to know everything from her waking life, but she knew it differently in sleep. I was very fond of her sleeping self.

Twenty-five years later, when I consulted Kathy in preparation for this book, she looked back on our experiments with quite a bit of surprise that she could have trusted me as much as she did to allow these goings-on. The events were not of enough importance to her that she has ever given them very much thought in the meantime, as I have. We have not had contact very often in the intervening years. As I see it, it was my awareness of her high degree of suggestibility and my automatic commitment not to infringe upon her privacy or to cause possible stress that restrained me from experimenting with Kathy more than I did. I always respected her fully in her sleeping state and shared our experiences with her in her waking state for the sake of propriety if nothing else. As I recall our relationship, we took integrity for granted and trusted each other intuitively. It was when Kathy started sharing secrets with me in her sleep that she had not shared in waking life that I felt it might be better for her if we did not continue our dream companionship. She probably felt it had gone far enough also. We would be parting soon anyway.

Ironically, the next-to-last sleeping communication that I have any record of in my scattered notes consisted of my telling Kathy, when I was sound asleep, to turn off her alarm before it went off and not to wake me up in the morning. It was a very naughty idea. I think that is the only time that Kathy ever heard me speak clearly in my sleep and speak directly to her. I had no memory at all of saying such a thing, but I believed Kathy about it, as she believed my accounts. Two months later we had gone our separate ways.

Kathy's husband has not paid attention to her dream talent, and so she does not know or really care if it has continued. When she had to walk the floors at night recently because of a painful muscle, she sometimes heard their teenage son calling out in his sleep as if he were playing basketball. She opened his door a few times and tried to engage him in conversation, wondering if by chance any of her children inherited her tendency. He would answer her overtures with very angry retorts like "Get out of here!" and "This is mine not yours!" She took the hint.

Kathy does not record or analyze her dreams, but she recalls them and enjoys them daily. She can return to favorite dreams. After her stepmother died of cancer a few years ago, Kathy dreamed her nineteenth birthday for the first time, shopping in downtown San Francisco on September 3, 1953, all over again. That was one of the happiest days that Kathy had ever spent with her stepmother, whom she loved very much.

Thomas De Quincey stated of his dreams, "minutest incidents of childhood, or forgotten scenes of later years, were often revived.... I *recognized* them instantly.... I feel assured that there is no such thing as an ultimate *forgetting*."[14] St. Augustine and J. W. Dunne would certainly agree. It is all permanent at once.

One person marks the passing of each moment in her sleeping mind and enjoys glimpses of the past. Another person has an inaccurate and flexible sense of time but gets glimpses of the future. Perhaps we are all both people in one, in our sleep, less bound by time than we usually think.

The Dream Machine

I haven't heard about popular dream teachers encouraging people to try to purposely break the time barrier in their dreams yet, and I hope they won't, but some teachers have been encouraging people to break through the space barrier in their dreams. This is striving for astral projection or out-of-body experiences. I have not had such an experience, and, as Huckleberry Finn complained, some people get down on a thing that they haven't even tried and don't know anything about. I did have a dream about the subject, though.

I dreamed that I went into a very beautiful savings and loan office in Santa Ana, paneled with rich woods and thickly carpeted. A small dark man was the only person in sight, and I felt that he was doing something dishonest. I asked him to make a photocopy of a paper for me, and he said that the machine was not available for use. I said "Let me just see what's going on back here!" and walked quickly to one of the large office rooms behind him. There I found that he was putting three-dimensional objects into the copy machine and trying to duplicate them in three dimensions. Just then a couple of secretaries appeared and saw what I saw; they screamed, "He's not allowed to do that! He'll break the machine!

The dream machine.

We knew this man's experiment could blow up the whole building.

That warning may not be true, but it's an idea I have. It seems to me that trying to manufacture unusual dream experiences may not be wise.

I have no explanation for the experience two friends of mine had about twenty-five years ago. They were college-age sisters sleeping in the same bed. Their mother heard them shouting and rushed in. They had both been dreaming that there was a black spider on the ceiling and that together they were trying to knock it down! There is no way to verify this report of mutual dreaming, but it comes from a highly intelligent and highly honest source.

In spite of my reluctance to experiment in out-of-body larks, I seem to have tried a rather crafty trick shortly after my dream about the savings and loan. I had read C. S. Lewis' interesting discussion of time travel and peering into a different time in *The Dark Tower.* There one of his characters remarked that "a man in 1938 can't get to 1939 in less than a year."[15]

In my dream William James seemed to have found a shorter way to get from one point to another in time or space. He felt that the distance from one point to another that has been given to us by authorities (a straight line) is obviously wrong, and that he and his colleagues could now overcome the artificial handicap of not knowing the shortest distance between two points. I'm pretty sure that James was talking about curved time and space and the true relationship that the dimensions have to each other, but by the time I finished my two-part dream I completely forgot what his solution was.[16]

Apparently James' idea inspired me to do something practical, and so in my dream I dialed Harper & Row in San Francisco with enthusiastic confidence and told the woman who answered that I wanted two points of information. I wanted "routine information." She understood. That was the first point. Second, I wanted a preview copy of my future book, *The Gift of Dreams,* which they would publish next year. She said that I could have one now and asked if I would also like an interview with the writer. I said no to that offer, thinking how ridiculous it was. If I knew the answers to the questions I have about how to finish the book, I wouldn't be asking for a preview copy to help me out.

Feeling that I had greatly simplified the rest of my work, I woke up. I have been slightly mystified ever since, and I am finishing the book the hard way. It was a nice try.

Notes

1. John Calvin, *Institutes of the Christian Religion (Philadelphia: Westminster, 1960), Volume I, XV.2. This is page 185 of the John T. McNeill edition in Library of Christian Classics.*
2. For a brief discussion of the possibility of children dreaming the inner experi-

ences of their parents, see the final chapter of Frances G. Wickes, *The Inner World of Childhood* (New York: Mentor, 1968).

3. P. D. Ouspensky, *A New Model of the Universe* (New York: Vintage Books, 1971), Chapter XI. On pp. 411–412 Ouspensky claims that in Matthew 19:28, properly translated from the Greek, Christ refers to life repetition.

4. Norman MacKenzie, *op. cit.,* p. 72.

5. Arthur Koestler, *op. cit.,* p. 183.

6. "Parapsychology: The Science of the Uncanny," *Newsweek,* March 4, 1974, pp. 57f.

7. C. S. Lewis, *The Discarded Image,* (Cambridge: Cambridge University Press, 1969), p. 89.

8. C. S. Lewis, *The Dark Tower* (London: Collins, 1977).

9. J. W. Dunne, *An Experiment with Time* (London: Purnell & Sons Limited, 1958).

10. J. Stafford Wright, *Man in the Process of Time* (Grand Rapids: Eerdmans, 1956), p. 56.

11. Morton Kelsey, *op. cit.,* p. 184.

12. Herman Melville, *Moby Dick,* chapter 14.

13. John Abercrombie, "Producing Dreams by Whispering," in *The New World of Dreams* by Woods and Greenhouse, p. 61.

14. Thomas De Quincey, *op. cit.,* p. 61.

15. C. S. Lewis, *The Dark Tower,* p. 19.

16. See Marilyn Ferguson's article "Karl Pribram's Changing Reality" in *Human Behavior* (May 1978, pp. 28–33). Pribram is a neuroscientist at Stanford University and author of *Languages of the Brain.* Ferguson describes Pribram's new belief that the brain is a hologram interpreting a holographic universe. If this theory is true, our brains mathematically construct what we perceive as reality by interpreting frequencies from a dimension beyond time and space that can be called quantum reality. This article does not mention dreams, but the implication is obvious; if Pribram is correct, dreams can bypass our normal, constricting perceptual mode and give us direct access to the realm of the frequency domain, which is a nonlinear dimension. There we are not bound by time and space. It was Synesius (circa 400 A.D.) who claimed to be inspired by God when he wrote "Nothing is so characteristic of dreams as to steal space and to create without time." (Quoted on p. 276 of Morton Kelsey's *Dreams; The Dark Speech of the Spirit.*)

JUNK DREAMS
AND JEWEL DREAMS:
OUR CREATIONS

Dreams are queer things.

C. S. Lewis, *unpublished letter to Arthur Greeves,* 1916

Dream Drudgery

One night when I was in the midst of the intense labor of writing this book, I awakened at 3 A.M. and realized that I had been scrubbing my mother's kitchen floor on my hands and knees. Only half awake, I was absolutely disgusted with such a waste of time. It's bad enough to try to keep one heavily trafficked house clean while working full time on a writing project, but to work in sleep as a scrublady in other people's houses in addition is outrageous. I could have been free-flying, a thrill I haven't had for years, or traveling, or enjoying other refreshment of spirit. When I recalled that the scrubwater had been ankle deep, I felt this was

136

the stupidest dream I ever had. I really resented it, considering that no one's floor profited from all my labor.

Later I checked my dream diary and discovered that scrubbing floors at night is an altruistic hobby of mine. I even scrubbed Catherine Hearst's kitchen floor once as a favor because her daughter Patty had been kidnapped. (Catherine was Kathryn, obviously.) I also voluntarily scrubbed and waxed an entire dance hall one night for a man I knew named Earl Cato (whose two names stand for high rank and public probity), who was passing out fried fish snacks to a crowd of dancers. (Neither Cato nor the dancers noticed the spectacular shine on that immense floor, but I still remember it. It shone like a dance floor in heaven.)

Because I failed to go back to sleep, I recalled that I had finally managed to get the kitchen floor clean and dry, and that then I had received a large, beautiful seashell sculpture from the South Pacific, mounted on spindly brass legs. I marveled at how much work it must have taken for native craftsmen to match three great shells and fit them together perfectly. But I had no place to use the sculpture and disliked the cheap looking little legs besides. I supposed I would store the thing in a closet.

It was certainly a junk dream until I thought it over a day and a half later. Then it became one of my jewel dreams. I decided that a small flood is still a flood, even on a kitchen floor. Floods are my life dream theme, and I have come to realize that they represent the deeper-than-conscious life. Suddenly this silly dream revealed how hard my unconscious mind is working along with my conscious mind on this book. (That reminds me of what Glenn Clark wrote about the unconscious mind working with the conscious mind just as the hind feet of a deer track with the front feet.)

I asked the dream what shells mean to me, and the answer was "gifts from the sea." In my life that means creative gifts from the unconscious. What would native craftsmanship be? My own hard work on the gift ideas to make them fit together into a pleasing pattern. Why the spindley legs? Because my dream ideas aren't based upon any recognized authority; they have to be offered on a humble basis. Nevertheless, they stand firm.

That was a good dream commentary on my writing this book

about dreams. It was mildly encouraging without making any big promises. It commented upon where some of my ideas have been coming from. It cheered me on.

Dreams of Genius

The most famous and beloved example of all junk creativity is the verse that author Dorothy Parker is often credited with writing in a dream. She awakened believing that her four-line poem was so wise and beautiful that it would reveal her to be the greatest poet and most profound thinker of all time. When she read her masterpiece the next day it said:

Hogamus Higamus
Men are Polygamous,
Higamus Hogamus
Women Monogamous.[1]

Another writer named Dale Eunson did even better. He dreamed he was the greatest poet of all time because he had written only one line of poetry, and in it he had revealed ultimate Truth to the human race. He recited his one line to an immense audience in a vast amphitheater, and they sat stunned with reverent awe. Then they arose, screaming with joy, and lifted Eunson to their shoulders. He awoke and hastily scribbled down the one line that made him the most profound writer who ever lived: "Oh, come see the deer, bighearted Oro."[2] In the light of day it was a bit of a let-down.

Another man, who was in fact illiterate, dreamed one night that he could suddenly compose magnificent poetry spontaneously. When he woke up, it was true. He became the first great poet of the English language. It is surprising how few people today know the story of Caedmon. He was a lay worker in a monastery at Whitby, England, in the second half of the seventh century. He was advanced in years and had never learned any poems or songs. Sometimes after dinner at the monastery they would all take turns singing at the harp to entertain each other. Caedmon would slip out before his turn came because he had no songs to share. One night he left for this reason and went to the stable because it was his turn to guard the cattle. He went to sleep, and in his dream a man came and commanded him, "Caedmon, sing me something."

Caedmon answered that if he could sing anything he would have stayed with his friends in the dining room. The man told him to sing anyway. Caedmon asked what he was supposed to sing, and the man told him to sing about the beginning of things. Caedmon promptly began to sing fine poetry in Old English, which in translation would be something like this:

Now shall we praise   the Prince of heaven,
The might of the Maker   and his manifold thought,
The work of the Father: of what wonders he wrought. . . .

Caedmon awoke and remembered his song well. He kept adding to it when he was awake, and the next morning he went to his manager and told him about the dream. He was taken to the abbess, Hilda, who summoned the wise and educated people of the community to hear the story and song. They all agreed that Caedmon had received a gift from God. They told him some other Christian teaching that they would like to have in poetic form and sent him home. The next morning Caedmon had a new poem for them. After that he was invited to become a monk and moved with his family into the monastery to practise his art. He was regularly taught the content of the Bible aloud in his own language, Old English, and he meditated upon the teaching and turned it into songs and poems that learned men came to write down. He put into poetry all of Genesis and the major stories and teachings of the entire Bible. He also wrote many other poems about the pains of hell, the bliss of heaven, and the judgment and mercy of God. Most of his poetry has been lost because of fires and other destruction through the centuries.

We have this story from the book that serves as our prime source of knowledge about Old English history, *Ecclesiastical History of the English People.* This book was completed in 731 by the first great scholar in England, the Venerable Bede, who wrote it in Latin. Bede was so close to the time of Caedmon and was such a reliable scholar that it is unfair to brush the story off as a superstitious fable. True or false, it sounds more credible than many well-accepted historical facts.

Surely the best known work of dream creativity in English literature is the poem "Kubla Khan" by Samuel Taylor Coleridge. In the summer of 1797 Coleridge fell asleep one day while reading some dull prose about a palace built by Kubla Khan in China about five hundred years earlier. He slept three hours, and images as real as life rose up before him, accompanied by at least two hundred or three hundred lines of poetry describing what he saw. When he awakened, he remembered the entire poem that had come to him and began to write it down. When he had recorded only fifty-four lines, a visitor arrived and stayed over an hour. As soon as the visitor left, Coleridge returned to his poem and found to his horror that all the rest was lost to his memory. He called the fifty-four lines only a fragment, but it has been one of the favorite poems in English literature. It begins:

In Xanadu did Kubla Khan
   A stately pleasure-dome decree;
Where Alph, the sacred river, ran
   Through caverns measureless to man
Down to a sunless sea. . . .

Freud insisted that, although people can produce foreign languages that they have studied better in dreams than in waking life, when people dream that they are composing prose or poetry they are deluded. People can't even create ordinary talk in their dreams, much less interesting literature. They are merely sticking together odd phrases they have come across in waking life, in random patterns. It seems strange indeed if Freud did not know about "Kubla Khan" and many lesser dream writings. He claimed in the 1933 edition of *The Interpretation of Dreams,* "analysis always shows us that the dream has merely taken the dream-thoughts fragments of speeches which have really been delivered or heard, and has dealt with them in the most arbitrary fashion."[3] Coleridge's experience alone would seem to refute such a generalization.

"Kubla Khan" was not all the poetry that Coleridge wrote in his sleep, just the best. The following dream-written epitaph ab-

breviates Coleridge to Col' and Edinburgh to E'nbro' and has not
become famous for obvious reasons:

Here lies at length poor Col' and with screaming,
Who died, as he had always lived, a dreaming:
Shot dead, while sleeping, by the gout within,
Alone, and all unknown, at E'nbro' in an Inn.

This dreadful verse by a fine poet is notable in that Coleridge
claimed in his dream that he was dreaming all his life. Not many
people say that in rhyme in their sleep.

When I was eighteen, I wrote what I considered a beautiful
poem in my sleep, and when I awakened only one unusual phrase
remained, along with the imagery and mood. I tried to recreate the
poem, realizing that my waking effort was an extremely inferior
copy of the original. I felt that the resulting verses were worth
keeping as a reminder of what the true poem had been like. This
is a reversal of the situation I have encountered more than once,
in which apparently real furniture or food in my dreams turn out
to be only cardboard when I handle them. Here is the cardboard
version of what was in my dream a real poem about great peace
and goodness in some other mode of existence:

Brown bees aglint with yellow sweetness,
Strong as sour, dark as gold,
Floating in the honeyed air-light
Purring decades, bumble-old.

Time, eclyptic, warm as syrup,
Light as skeins of tissue-silk
Soft unwinding, slipping downward,
Intimate as trickling milk.

Colors white as cream and ivory,
Folds of fabric mute and clear;
Faint cretonne of ecru curtains
Hanging warm and wondrous-sheer.

There above a floorless aeon,
There behind a vacant throne,
Somewhere in the subtle fullness
Glimmer bees that drone and drone.

Funny Trains of Thought

I have only retained one literary dream creation of mine in its entirety, and it seems to be extremely unusual if not especially good. Although one can read many accounts of people writing funny things in their sleep and taking them seriously, I have never found an account elsewhere of someone purposely writing something funny in a dream and thinking it was funny. This occurred when I was an adult but had not yet tried writing anything very whimsical or witty and did not believe that I had that ability. In my dream I was setting the table and made up a very clever bit of light verse about something on the table. It delighted and amazed me. I tried to do it again and came out with a second verse on a different topic entirely. The cumulative impact of the two original jokes struck me so funny that I laughed so hard I woke myself up. I could remember every word of the second verse and not one thing about the first. This is the second humorous verse that popped out of my mouth:

Some people chew tobacco-stuff;
I don't, 'cause I'm not up to snuff.

Late in 1972 I dreamed that I was filling in a long questionnaire and spontaneously dashed off an unusually creative answer to each of the routine questions. I marveled at the ease with which I had filled the page with clever wordplay and imaginative insights. I am convinced that this spurt of creativity was at least partly true, not a mere delusion as Freud would have assumed. I awakened with one of the answers still in my mind; I have no idea what the question was. My answer was, "Sometimes when a train of thought comes by, I hop aboard and ride it to its destination. I just hope God is my conductor." Because of my interest in brain physiology, I knew right away that this bit of wordplay was referring to the fact that our thoughts are electrical impulses in our physical brains, which must be conducted, as well as to the fact that God is the best guide on our mental journeys.

Richard A. Underwood, author of the essay "Myth, Dream, and Contemporary Philosophy," shared a favorite dream of his about his mental journey. It caused him to awaken laughing out loud.

He was writing his Ph.D. dissertation, which reflected upon the religious and philosophical significance of the understanding of the word as creative utterance, by way of such figures as C. G. Jung and Martin Heidegger. His dream was a view of a town square with a fountain in the middle. The fountain went dry. Then it became a fountain of flame. Bedlam ensued as townspeople shouted out of upstairs windows and out of doorways, and others shouted and ran about the fountain in every direction. All their words appeared as streams of letters instead of sounds. The words flooded the square and put out the fire, then drowned the people. "The dream ended, as it had begun, with no signs of life, except for an occasional person bobbing up, gasping for breath, seeking in vain to extricate himself from the sea of words in which he was drowning."[4] Underwood said that after he stopped laughing he began to take the dream as a serious personal evaluation.

Underwood was secure enough to take the sardonic dream comment about his pursuits in good spirit and profit from it. In contrast, *The Psychiatric Dictionary* by Hinzie and Campbell mentions that when patients dream in response to urgent demands from their psychiatrists for dream accounts the resulting dreams often express a derisive attitude toward the analyst. There is no hint here that the humorous depiction could be an astute comment the analyst would do well to consider. Some of the serious statements by psychiatrists in that very dictionary may well elicit intelligent derision. For example:

The illogicality of a dream does not *necessarily* mean that the patient himself is illogical in his waking life [italics added].

Thus a dream that ends with a bell ringing *when the ringing of an alarm clock wakes the sleeper* is ... to protect the sleeper from disturbances [italics added].

Sometimes part of a dream is regarded during the dream state as having been dreamed; the dreamer therefore does not consider that the dream within a dream belongs to the dream. He continues to dream, looking upon the continuation only as the real dream. "The inclusion of a certain content in 'a dream within a dream' is therefore equivalent to the wish that what has been characterized as a dream had never occurred."[5]

Like many statements *in* dreams, these are more or less preposterous, though the authors assumed that they were making good sense. Could it be that their own unconscious minds are expressing derisive attitudes toward their conscious work by sabotoging it?

According to Arthur Koestler there are three major areas of creativity: humor, science, and art. Scientific and artistic creativity occur in dreams, but no doubt humorous creativity is most common because dreams are laden with puns. As Koestler has pointed out in *The Act of Creation,* in a pun two strings of thought are tied together by the knot of a similar sound. Punning is a form of creativity related to rhyming.

The worst dream pun I ever created came at the end of an utterly shoddy dream. I met a man named Danny Orlis (the boy hero of a series of children's books by Bernard Palmer), and then everything went wrong. The buses were not on schedule, my typewriter typed wrong letters, my family ruined my best towels, and my husband would not share the car with me. I noticed that our yard had a very large evergreen tree growing horizontally right across the lawn. "We need to *spruce up* the yard," I said seriously.

Sometimes the dream pun is only acted out, not stated. A few months after a friend of mine was sexually abused by a married man with a Spanish name, he tried to trick her in court by having an actor pose in his place. This is a ploy that the law allows. Right after hearing of Karen's latest courtroom trauma, I dreamed I had to identify one man from a group of nine, but I didn't know who or why. One fellow raised his hand and grinned, "Am I the man? I'm Juan Pecan." I said no. Another man called out, "Am I the one? I'm Pablo Walnut." I said no and thought, "These aren't real names. What's going on?" Then the doorbell awakened me. The dream was broken off, but I realized what it had been about. It was an elaborate pun exclaiming, "What kind of a nut is Karen's rapist?" This dream cheered me and cheered Karen.

Most people hate bad puns, but few people realize that they can be triggered by activity of a certain tiny spot in the brain. Forster's syndrome is a brain disorder that is manifested by compulsive punning. In 1929 a German surgeon named Forster was removing a brain tumor. Whenever he manipulated the spot where the tumor was located, the conscious patient started in with whatever words the surgeon had just uttered and ran that on into a string of somewhat appropriate although grizzly puns concerning the surgery!

As eccentric and humble as puns are, they are the epitome of creativity. The pun combines elements that were already known separately in an unexpected relationship. That is what all human creativity and problem solving does. Contemporary scientist and thinker Jacob Bronowski says that creation exists in finding unity, finding likenesses, and finding pattern. "The discoveries of science, the works of art are explorations—more, are explosions, of a hidden likeness."[6]

Scientific Dreams

The most famous account of dream activity in the area of science and technology is that of Friedrich August von Kekulé, professor of chemistry in Ghent, Belgium, who fell asleep and dreamed one afternoon in 1865. Kekulé's dream discovery is said to be one of the cornerstones of modern science, perhaps the most brilliant piece of prediction in the whole range of organic chemistry. It was the discovery of the ring structure of the molecules of certain organic compounds. Kekulé told the story as follows:

"I turned my chair to the fire and dozed. Again the atoms were gambolling before my eyes. This time the smaller groups kept modestly in the background. My mental eye, rendered more acute by repeated visions of this kind, could now distinguish larger structures, of manifold conformation; long rows, sometimes more closely fitted together; all twining and twisting in snakelike motion. But look! What was that? One of the snakes had seized hold of its own tail, and the form whirled mockingly before my eyes. As if by a flash of lightning I awoke.... Let us learn to dream, gentlemen."[7]

Elias Howe invented the sewing machine, after a long struggle, by dreaming that he was being attacked by tribal warriors wielding unusual spears. The spears had holes near their points. When Howe awoke he realized that sewing machine needles would have to have thread holes near their points.

Linus Pauling, contemporary winner of the Nobel Prize in chemistry, says that the unconscious mind cannot be forced. Problems can only be suggested to it. He says he thinks about a scientific problem in bed while awaiting sleep. In a few weeks or months the germ of a solution may come into his mind.

Otto Loewi was aided by his sleeping mind more tardily but more dramatically than Pauling. In 1903 he got the idea that an electric impulse of a nerve may trigger a chemical action that acts on a muscle or gland, but he did not know how to test the theory and left the idea dormant for seventeen years. During the night before the day before Easter Sunday in 1920 he awakened and jotted a few notes on a slip of paper, then returned to sleep. When he got up at 6 A.M. he recalled having an important idea but could not decipher his scrawl. On Easter Sunday at 3 A.M. he awakened with the same idea again. This time he did not take a chance. He got up and performed his dream experiment right then on a frog heart that was in his laboratory; he proved the chemical transmission of nerve impulses. In 1936 he received the Nobel Prize for that discovery.

Humorist H. Allen Smith tells in his memorable essay "Notes in the Night," which is now reprinted in *The Best of H. Allen Smith,* that Oliver Wendell Holmes, the physician and author, dreamed that he had discovered a great truth when he was trying ether on himself in an experiment. Amnesia immediately destroyed the insight. Holmes arranged to take ether again with a stenographer present to record the great truth if his dream came back to him. The words he spoke to the stenographer were, "The entire universe is permeated with a strong odor of turpentine!" It was a big disappointment. I still remembered that story many years later when I read once in *Science News* that some scientists have found that the entire universe is permeated with a strong odor of ammonia. I couldn't help wondering if Holmes had meant to say ammonia, or if the odor of the ether had combined with the odor of ammonia in his dream to create the impression of the odor of turpentine.

Contemporary mathematician Jaques Hadamard, author of *The Psychology of Invention in the Mathematical Field,* has claimed, "One phenomenon is certain and I can vouch for its absolute certainty: the sudden and immediate appearance of a solution at the very moment of sudden awakening. On being very abruptly awakened by an external noise, a solution long searched for appeared to me at once without the slightest instant of reflection on my part—the fact was remarkable enough to have struck me unforgettably—and in a quite different direction from any of those which I had previously tried to follow."[8]

Albert Einstein's best ideas are said to have come into his mind right after he got up. The French philosopher Condorcet solved a mathematical equation in his sleep. William Blake received a truly improved method of copper engraving in a dream in which he was instructed by his dead brother. A great engineer named James Brindley was said to go to bed when he had a difficult problem and to stay there several days until it was solved.

Another strange story is that of nineteenth-century naturalist Louis Agassiz, which he told in his book *Recherches Sur Les Poissons Fossiles.* He was once working to free a fossil fish from its stone bed, but gave up and left it. A few nights later he dreamed he saw the fish swimming about alive. He checked the fossil later, and it did not resemble his dream. The dream came back again, and again he failed to see how it related to the fossil. The third time that he had the dream, he made a sketch of his dream fish afterward. Using his sketch as a blueprint, he tried to free the fossil again. A layer of stone fell away when he chipped at it, revealing an exact replica of his drawing. This was a unique specimen of a species then unknown.

Contemporary biologist Garrett Hardin may or may not value dreams, but he has claimed that two elements that are needed to produce any creative genius are irresponsibility and alienation. When those qualities combine with pertinence and comprehensibility, valuable insights can come out of our dreams.

It is my own unsubstantiated opinion that some of our strange childhood dreams, particularly those that come when we are fevered, are actual perceptions of some aspects of the nature of force and matter. If brilliant physicists had some of those dreams while working on problems such as radiation-dominated versus matter-dominated eras, the "deuterium bottlenecks," primordial black holes, quantum processes, quarks and gluons, superparticles, supergravity, and the mysteries of shadow physics, I suspect that they could have some dream insights like that of Kekulé.

After all, Michael Faraday, one of the great physicists of all time, had waking perceptions that seem distinctly dreamlike. He *saw* the stresses surrounding magnets and electric currents as curves in space. He saw the universe patterned by narrow tubes through which all forms of energy radiations are propagated. A self-educated man from an extremely humble background, absolutely ignorant of advanced mathematics, Faraday invented the electric engine, developed the first dynamo, discovered electromagnetic induction, and formulated laws of electrolysis. His achievement required the highest powers of mathematical analysis, but Faraday did it with visual intuition instead of mathematics.

Surely this visionary genius was a manifestation of the powers of the right hemisphere of the brain running ahead of the left, as happens to us in our dream life.

Once when I was reading an article about astronomy to see what it said about black holes, I was shocked by recognition of the nightmare that had haunted my illnesses when I was a child. The dream came in various indescribable forms, but it was always the same in essence. I might find myself in an absolutely static setting as simple as a picture in the simplest coloring book for toddlers. There were tons of tension in each square foot of flat space. There would be one small object present, like a stiff little flower on an expanse of flat lawn by a flat path. This object would become a horror to me, because in that lifeless, breezeless place that inert object might unleash power like a million hydrogen bombs at once. Another version of this was the spinning of a turntable in a way that consumed or dissolved or expanded all that is.

Another version was as if all the sounds of music, all the sounds there are in the world, came closer and closer to one pure note. And when they had all merged into one pure, flat tone, that note narrowed and became more pure until it was just one tiny *eeeeeeee* that I could barely hear. And all the pressures of spheres so immense that I could not even see the edges of them pressed me practically out of existence; it was like having planets vastly larger than earth converge upon my small head. Yet all these incomprehensibly gigantic bodies were in fact compressed into that one barely audible *eeeeeeee*. All the mass and potency there is, which is hell to have to encounter for a young human brain, had been sucked or compressed into that pinpoint of sound.

New Light For Inner Landscapes

The mystery in a fevered brain is dreadful mystery, but to encounter mystery in health is an essential of full human living. Einstein said that the most beautiful thing we can experience is the mysterious, the source of all true art and science. One who no longer pauses to wonder and stand in awe, is as good as dead; his eyes are closed. It is Rollo May's opinion that the value of dreams is not their gift of specific answers to things but their ability to open up new areas of psychic reality, to shake us out of our customery ruts, and to throw new light on segments of our lives. Similarly, film artist Ingmar Bergman has said that the dream can give us new thoughts, new ways of thinking and feeling. "It can give you a new light for your inner landscape."[9]

An outstanding example of a new light for inner landscapes is the poem *Piers the Plowman,* which consists of three mysterious dream visions and their allegorical interpretations about human life, the individual, and society. The poem has grim humor and calls humanity back to Christian ideals. The poem was written six hundred years ago. Although it is usually attributed to a William Langland, we know almost nothing about its authorship, much less whether it was really based upon dream experiences or not.

Synesius of Cyrene, the early fifth century bishop who wrote the first outstanding Christian book about dreams, claimed that dreams come especially to minds given to the love of wisdom, to enlighten them. Furthermore, dreams often helped him with his writing by putting his ideas in order and improving his style. When his writing became too pompous, his dreams corrected him. He spent most of his life among books or out hunting, and he found that his dreams sometimes told him clever ways to catch elusive animals. He also spent three rather unhappy years as an ambassador, and his dreams guided him safely through that experience, even enabling him to speak boldly before the Roman emperor.

Synesius is not the only author who has been aided by dreams. Jerome Cardan, a sixteenth-century Italian philosopher, claimed that he kept dreaming in detail the plan and subject matter of a large book. He finally decided to write the book, and the dreams continued until the book was published. Goethe said that many of his poems first came to him in dreams. Voltaire dreamed a whole canto of his work *La Henriade.* Sir Walter Scott told a friend, "The half-hour between waking and rising has all my life proved propitious to any task which was exercising my invention. . . . It was always when I first opened my eyes that the desired ideas thronged upon me."[10]

Charlotte Brontë had immense success with a technique that is being tried by many people today. When she needed to write in her novels about experiences that were unfamiliar to her, she would think about that need many nights just before going to sleep. Eventually, perhaps weeks later, she would wake up one day knowing about the experiences that she needed to describe.

The eighteenth-century composer Guiseppe Tartini dreamed that he bargained with Satan, who played him the most perfect music he had ever heard. When he awakened, he could not recall any of it except one trill. He used that as the theme for what is considered his best work, *The Devil's Trill.* The early nineteenth-century English poet Thomas Hood had a different kind of diabolic dream. In his case it came after the performance of the only play he ever wrote, *Tragedy of My Tragedy.* The performance was indeed a tragedy. That night Hood dreamed that he watched the entire play again in a theater full of devils. He was being damned for the sins of authorship! He never tried writing drama again.

Alfred, Lord Tennyson wrote an unusual poem that never saw print; he told Lewis Carroll about it. He dreamed a very long poem, all about fairies, which began with very long lines. The lines got shorter and shorter until the poem ended with fifty or sixty lines of two syllables each! He thought the poem was excellent, but he couldn't remember a bit of it when he awakened.

A client of the late Jungian analyst Max Zeller, who practised in Los Angeles, dreamed one night that he sang a part in a performance of the opera *The Woman without a Shadow,* although he had never heard the music in waking life. He laughed when he told his analyst that he had to sing it in the key of "B natural." That story interested me when I encountered it, because in a recent dream I had sung the lead in a public performance of *Hello Dolly,* although I don't know one thing about that musical except its title and had never heard the music. I remembered that fact during my dream and thought, "The reason I know all this is that I've been singing it in my sleep." I then woke up and recalled that in my dream I had changed the title to *Novello Dolly,* which I thought better. It was novel, no doubt. I suppose that I invented the entire score as I went along, orchestra in tow.

An author friend of mind, Gracia Fay Ellwood, composed an aphorism for me in one of my dreams, after serving as hostess for a Valentine tea for women of the AAUW all afternoon. During the extremely long and peculiar meeting one of the women had asked me rudely what difference it made that my husband was a history teacher, and I answered that it was important to me right now because I was busy writing a book about dreams and his background helped me. At 6 P.M. I excused myself as the meeting droned on endlessly and thanked Gracia Fay for her hospitality. She was in the kitchen with her husband Robert, who had come home by then. She looked me in the eye and declared with feeling, "Repetition outwanes the capacity of the poor, but does not fulfill the propensity of the rich. *Remember that!*" I did.

Immediately after recording that dream I fell asleep and dreamed that the appropriate response to Gracia Fay's words of wisdom would have been, "Sages are people who are aurorally awakening." This seemed such an extremely clever multifaceted pun when I dreamed it that I woke right up, and I have been trying to figure it out ever since. The message was set in a desert sunrise where Aurora was casting her light across the sagebrush. I knew that the word sages might have referred to Gracie Fay but that it most definitely referred to St. Basil. Perhaps the fact that Gracia Fay was cooking meat during our exchange and the fact that both sage and basil are herbs used for flavoring meat was part of the wordplay.

A few months later I learned to my surprise that Karl Barth, whom I have never studied at all, is called the sage of Basel (Switzerland). I knew in my bones that this was a key to my too-clever dream pun. Later I read Clark Pinnock's statement, "Together with the fathers of the church, Barth saw that the heart of the gospel lay in the gracious decision of the triune God to reconcile fallen humankind and restore a ruined creation through the person and work of Jesus Christ."[11] That seems to me to link Barth and Basil, since Basil is a father of the church and one who ascertained that God is triune.

Because Barth was Swiss, I became suspicious that he was probably in the third act of my great Swiss theology and psychology extravaganza. I checked back in my dream diary and discovered that months earlier the long, complex Swiss musical pageant had actually occurred a night or two after the horrendous pun about sages. Karl Barth must have been mixed up in both of them.

I still had no idea that Karl Barth cared about either music or dreams. Later I read that Barth especially loved the music of Mozart but was bothered by the fact that Mozart rejected Protestantism in favor of Catholicism because Protestantism seemed too intellectual and rationalistic to him. Thomas Merton reflected in his book *Conjectures of a Guilty Bystander* about Karl Barth's account of a dream in which he had to give Mozart a theology examination. Barth had tried to structure the questions so that Mozart would do as well as possible, but to his dismay Mozart refused to answer a word.

Merton was deeply moved by Barth's account of the dream, because he perceived that it was about Barth's own salvation. Merton was obviously taking into account the fact that Mozart was one of the greatest child prodigies who ever lived and died in his mid-thirties, still at the height of his highly intuitive creative power. Merton interpreted Barth's dream about the silent Mozart to be a dream about the silent indwelling Christ.

Merton wrote, "Fear not, Karl Barth! Trust in the divine mercy. Though you have grown up to become a theologian, Christ remains a child in you. Your books (and mine) matter less than we might think! There is a Mozart in us who will be our salvation."[12] Ironically, Merton and Barth left their books and realized their salvation on the same day, December 10, 1968.

Probably "Sages are people who are aurorally awakening" will never do more for me than slightly increasing my interest in Karl Barth, because it is too far-fetched and obscure. But my friend Dr. Alice Bergel created a superb dream aphorism that made great sense to her personally. One morning in the spring of 1978 she awakened with the following words on her lips: "Enjoy the few hours of *helios* before the dark comes in." Being a scholar, she knew that *helios* is Greek for sun. Being one who once lost almost everything when she fled Nazi Germany, she knew how darkness can come in. Being technically retired but very active, she knows that she is in a delightful phase of life. "I'm doing it!" she said six months later. She is enjoying her hours of *helios* more consciously now.

Stevenson the Dreamer

There is probably no author who has left so unusual an account of his creative dreaming as Robert Louis Stevenson. He described dreaming as the small theatre of the brain which we keep brightly lighted all night long."[13] He was his own dream laboratory. There are some among us, he observed, who can claim to have lived longer and more richly than their neighbors because they are still active when they lie asleep. For such people the treasures of memory include a rich harvest of dreams. Stevenson began as an ardent and uncomfortable dreamer when he was a young child, suffering utterly terrible nightmares during his frequent illnesses. As an older child he took long journeys in his sleep, visiting many places, and spent a great deal of time visiting Georgian England in the clothing of that period. He began to read in his dreams, stories so vivid and moving that no books in real life ever satisfied him again.

A law student in waking life, Stevenson went through a period in college when he spent every night as a surgical student who worked on hideous bodies all day and then climbed endless gloomy stairs in soaking wet clothes all night in his dreams. The strain of these gruelling nights as a surgical student finally sent Stevenson to a real doctor, and some medication ended the whole series permanently.

It was when Stevenson turned to writing as a way to earn a living that his dream life became more extraordinary. He had long had the habit of making up stories in bed as a way to go to sleep. As a writer he automatically began to structure his story ideas before he went to sleep in an attempt to produce products that he could eventually sell. When he did this, the stories in his dreams began to take better literary form also. It seemed as if he had an unseen collaborator trying hard to work out stories in his sleep to help him pay his bills. He admitted that, sometimes when he awoke with the cry "I have it, that'll do!" upon his lips, eager to work on the new story with his waking mind, he found it to be a tissue of absurdities that couldn't be used. But all in all, he claimed, his night worker did half his work for him. He took the dream productions and improved the shape some, dressed them in good sentences, sat at a table and used a pen, and got the manuscripts mailed. He said that sitting at the table was about the worst part of being a writer. He described in detail how he had failed in his waking attempts to write a story about the double nature of man's being and how *The Strange Case of Dr. Jekyll and Mr. Hyde* finally came to him in a dream. For some reason that I don't know, philosopher Henri Bergson claimed that Stevenson had reached such a state by this time that he didn't know whether he was asleep or awake.

Stevenson said that once his many story composing dreams began the only other dreams he had were the delightful reading of wonderful books that don't exist in real life and delightful journeys to unknown lands. Like Dag Hammarskjöld, he would return to one place in particular again and again, every few months or years, "finding new field-paths, visiting new neighbors, beholding that happy valley under new effects of noon and dawn and sunset."[14] Stevenson died of tuberculosis in his early forties, but perhaps he did live as long as his neighbors in his own way.

C. S. Lewis the Dreamer

C. S. Lewis is well known as one of the most popular literary creators of our century. The fact that he led a very active dream life is less known.

Lewis once likened the pruning and polishing of creative ideas from his unconscious to the clear-headed waking evaluation of dream material. In his essay "On Criticism" Lewis observed that a very large part of the creative material that comes up from the unconscious and seems attractive and important in the early stages of planning a book actually needs to be discarded long before the book is finished. That is like the fact that people who are not bores tell us only about dreams that are in some way interesting by the standards of the waking mind, he said. In *The Personal Heresy* Lewis speculated about what makes an item interesting, and his remarks can be applied perfectly to dreams. Things may be interesting because they are so funny, because they are so true, because they are so unexpected, because they do just what we were expecting so well, because they carry us away from daily life into such fine regions of fantasy, or because they bring us back to our immediate surroundings with such a home-felt sense of reality.[15]

Lewis did consider his own dreams interesting enough to share with others or to record in his diary sometimes. As a young man he wrote to his friend Arthur Greeves once that he wished Arthur and his family would have the goodness to keep out of Lewis' dreams; he expected Arthur to remember his dream of the two of them and a relative walking along North Street when Lewis saw a ghost that the other two did not see. Later, he dreamed that he was walking with the other two in town again, and this time the place had been captured by Germans. They were hurrying along in terror through deserted streets with German soldiers always just about to catch them and do something terrible.

Another time he reported to Arthur that he had had a nightmare that Arthur might want to use in his writing. Lewis' foster mother, Mrs. Moore, used to hire a poor old woman named Mrs. Lovell to do odd jobs at their house. Mrs. Lovell eventually disappeared. Lewis dreamed that he went to a cupboard in the kitchen to look for something, and a heavy thing wrapped in brown paper dropped out at his feet. Picking it up and unwinding it, he found —Mrs. Lovell's head! That is reminiscent of Jung's statement in *Psychology and Alchemy* that the unconscious is always . . . the skeleton in the cupboard of perfection.

One of Lewis' best-known dreams is the one in which he was

sitting on Magdalen Bridge at dusk and then walked up a hill with some people. At the top there was a window in the air, and a lamb was slain and talked with the voice of a man. This dream came long before Lewis' conversion. Later the same year Lewis dreamed that he and a friend received a coffin, which was sent to them with a corpse in it for them to care for. The corpse was conscious, had some power of movement, and would not decay. It was as vivid as life. It got loose from its coffin and ran amok. It pursued the horrified Lewis into an elevator in a London subway.

In another dream, one that Lewis described to his father in 1927, he was walking among the valleys of the moon, a world of pure white rock, all deep chasms and spidery crags, with a perfectly black sky overhead. It was pure mineral solitude. Then Lewis saw, very far off, coming to meet him down a narrow ravine, a straight, tall figure, draped in black. "One knew it would be nicer not to meet that person: but one never has any choice in a dream, and for what seemed about an hour I went on till this stranger was right beside me."[16] The stranger closed a metal ring with a sharp interior around Lewis's wrist, cutting him to the bone. Then, without a word, he began to lead Lewis off down the same long valley from which he had come. Lewis said it was the desolate sense of being on the moon that permeated the dream.

Later Lewis was to have a dream about his deceased father. In his opinion at that time most dreams about the dead portrayed the dead either as still alive, fooling the dreamer, or else as bogies. However, in his dream he knew perfectly well that his father had died and yet was talking to him normally in their old dining room. He purposely touched his father, who felt warm and solid. Lewis said to his father, "But of course this body must be only an appearance. You can't really have a body now," and his father agreed cheerfully; then they talked about other topics. Lewis went to Arthur's house nearby and was bringing Arthur over to see his father, explaining the situation. Exactly at the place where an increased crunching under the wheels informed people that they had passed onto the gravel drive, at the study corner of the Lewis home, Arthur said in a voice of suppressed anxiety, "Oh no, Jack. It's just that you've been thinking about him and you've *imagined* he's there." Arthur's words shattered the cozy pleasantness of the dream and made Lewis realize that talking to a dead man is a horrible-sounding experience to most people. He awakened in terror.[17]

Lewis confided to his friend Dom Bede Griffiths that his memories of World War I haunted his dreams for years. On the morning of Palm Sunday in 1940 Lewis was dazed for hours by two bad dreams that do not sound very bad in the telling now. In one he was an ordinary soldier again, assigned as an aid to T. E. Bleiben; Bleiben was not an army officer, in fact, but his own parish priest. In the other he was in a large crowd that was becoming terrified, and he did not know the cause of the terror until he realized it as he awakened. It was the last day.

Not all of Lewis' remembered dreams were disturbing. Once he saw fit to write to Arthur, "I had the most vivid, tranquil dream about you the other night, just chatting in the old way."[18] And Lewis was interested in the dreams of his friends. He wrote to Owen Barfield in 1940 that he always remembered a certain dream that Barfield had shared with him once.

Those who are familiar with Lewis' fiction know that dreams come into it time after time. His dream of being doomed on the moon may or may not have colored his short story "Forms of Things Unknown." But dreams play a definite part in *The Pilgrim's Regress,* the science-fiction trilogy, *The Great Divorce,* the Narnian Chronicles, and *Till We Have Faces.* In Lewis' fiction even bad dreams would have good purposes.

My personal favorite of all of Lewis' poems is accidentally titled "Reason" in Lewis' collected short poems; it should be called "Reason and Imagination." Lewis described *reason* as symbolized by the goddess Athene, a virgin on a hilltop in heavenly light, giving us clear sight. Lewis described *imagination* as symbolized by the goddess Demeter, "Warm, dark, obscure and infinite, daughter of Night." Imagination's dim exploring touch is very different from reason's clear sight. "The beauty of her eyes with sleep/ Is loaded, and her pains are long, and her delight."[19] Her pains are those of fertility and motherhood. The point of the poem is that Lewis needs both kinds of knowing, the height of reason and the depth of imagination, in order to encounter full truth. There is no question that in this polarity Lewis was expressing much of what we learned later about the functions of the right and left hemispheres of the brain. He would almost surely have agreed that when he talked about imagination he meant visions, intuition, and dreams.

Lewis wrote in a letter once, "The imagination man in me is older, more continuously operative, and in that sense more basic than either the religious writer or the critic .... And it was, of course, he who has brought me, in the last few years, to write the series of Narnian stories for children."[20]

In describing his writing of the Narnian series, Lewis said that he was well into the story before Aslan, the great lion, came bounding in of his own accord, and took over the story. He didn't know exactly how that happened. He only knew that he had been having many dreams about lions just then.

The Genius of Dreams

Few people can use dream creativity as an aid in magnificant scientific or artistic endeavors, because few people are deeply involved in science and art. But all people have problems to solve and areas where growth is needed in their lives, and dreams seem to be able to help. William C. Dement, in *Some Must Watch While Some Must Sleep,* described an exploration into the phenomenon of problem solving in dreams at Stanford University. The experiment had several drawbacks, but it did show that, when over a thousand attempts were made to solve an unusual thought problem for fifteen minutes before students went to sleep, in seven instances the correct answer was then revealed in a dream and understood the next morning. There were two other cases in which dreams revealed the answers, but those were not counted because those subjects had actually solved the problem before going to sleep and then dreamed the answer as well. There were other subjects whose dreams that night referred to the correct answer, but the subjects did not connect the dream answers with the thought problems when they awakened, although they remembered the dreams.

Dement quoted Nobel Prize–winner in physiology and medicine Albert Szent-Gyorgyi, who said, "My work is not finished when I leave my workbench in the afternoon. I go on thinking about my problems all the time, and my brain must continue to think about them when I sleep because I wake up, sometimes in the middle of the night, with answers to questions that have been puzzling me."[21] I recall waking up once in the middle of the night with a picture in my mind of where my lost keys were. I did not recall the incident until the middle of the next afternoon. I went right to the spot, a box in a closet, and there were the keys. I had put them there myself by accident without knowing it.

Professional golfer Jack Nicklaus claimed in 1964 that he had learned how to correct the way he held his club in a dream and radically improved his game. One writer claimed that a dream told her how to get rid of her morning headaches by not arising so abruptly after her alarm went off. William C. Dement himself told how a realistic dream took him through extensive tests demonstrating in detail that he had lung cancer that had spread to his lymph nodes. The fact that he would never get to see his children grow up because he had failed to quit smoking caused him incredible anguish, which was exquisitely relieved when he awakened and realized it had been a dream. He quit smoking immediately. Alas, he began smoking again after two years of abstinence and said he needed another vivid dream to force him to quit again. Catherine Marshall has told of a friend of hers, a young housewife, who was enabled to quit smoking by a less medical, more religious dream.

My friend Elizabeth Waggoner needed to take a plate of fruit to a church luncheon one day in 1978. The night before she dreamed that she created a stunning effect by scooping melon balls from cantaloupe and honeydew pieces and filling the orange holes with green balls and green holes with orange balls. She tried it for fun, exactly as the dream had directed, and it delighted everyone. When friends asked her where she had found such a pretty idea, she had fun telling them how she had "dreamed it up," in perfect detail. She had never heard of such dream creativity before this experience.

Bishop Synesius advised, "Then let us all deliver ourselves to the interpretation of dreams, men and women, young and old, rich and poor, private citizens and magistrates, inhabitants of the town and of the country, artisans and orators. There is not any privileges, neither by sex, neither by age, nor fortune or profession. Sleep offers itself to all: it is an oracle always ready, our infallible and silent counselor."[22]

Lest anyone turn to our "infallible and silent" counselor too hastily and carelessly, I should add that once, when my husband and I were searching the used car lots for what was to be our family transportation for the next few years, I dreamed of one of the cars we were considering. I simply saw it in my dream, looking important. I wondered if that was advice to buy the car, but I did not know how to work with dreams in those days. We did not think it would be wise to be influenced by the dream; I don't know if it slightly increased our interest in that car or not. We were most influenced by the fact that this car was sold to us by a Christian who convinced us that it was in excellent condition. We remembered him every time we were stranded on roadsides with a crying baby and a hyperactive preschooler. After that experience we are even more opposed to presumptuous reliance upon dreams as oracles. If we had based our dreadful choice on my noncommital dream, we would have felt like superstitious fools as well as exploited customers. Dreams certainly may contribute to making good choices sometimes, but Synesius was advising us to learn to interpret our dreams rightly, not to follow them recklessly. Some of our problems are vastly more important than selection of a decent automobile. Admiral William S. Sims used to tell of a famous English admiral who kept dreaming that he knew the way to end the First World War. He could never remember the answer in the morning, and so the war went on. Finally he succeeded in forcing himself to write down the solution during the night. The way to end the war, according to his dream note, was "The skin is mightier than the banana." It didn't help a bit.

We win some and we lose some with dream creativity, just as with waking creativity. It pays to be flexible and keep trying.

Over a century ago F. W. Hildebrandt, Freud's favorite source on dreams until his own book came out, stated the positive side of creative dreaming this way:

... there are few of us who could not affirm, from our own experience, that there emerges from time to time in the creations and fabrics of the genius of dreams a depth and intimacy of emotion, a tenderness of feeling, a clarity of vision, a subtlety of observation, and a brilliance of wit such as we should never claim to have at our permanent command in our waking lives. There lies in dreams a marvelous poetry, an apt allegory, an incomparable humour, a rare irony. A dream looks upon the world in a light of strange idealism and often enhances the effects of what it sees by its deep understanding of their essential nature. It pictures earthly beauty to our eyes in a truly heavenly splendour and clothes dignity with the highest majesty, it shows us our everyday fears in the ghastliest shape and turns our amusement into jokes of indescribable pungency. And sometimes, when we are awake and still under the full impact of an experience like one of these, we cannot but feel that never in our life has the real world offered us its equal.[23]

Notes

1. H. Allen Smith, "Notes in the Night" in *The Best of H. Allen Smith* (New York: Trident Press, 1972), p. 370. Smith attributes the verse to Mrs. Amos Pinchott. (Stuart Holroyd, in *Dream Worlds,* quotes the verse with the couplets reversed and attributes it to William James, p.79.)

2. *Ibid.,* p. 378.

3. Leland E. Hinzie and Robert J. Campbell, *The Psychiatric Dictionary* (London: Oxford University Press, 1970), p. 234.

4. Richard A. Underwood, "Myth, Dream, and Contemporary Philosophy" in *Myth, Dreams and Religion,* edited by Joseph Campbell (New York: Dutton, 1970), p. 226.

5. Leland E. Hinzie and Robert J. Campbell, *op. cit.,* pp. 233–234.

6. Arthur Koestler, *op. cit.,* p. 200.

7. *Ibid.,* p. 118.

8. *Loc. cit.* For an especially vivid story of a mathematician solving a complex problem in his sleep, read the account by neurophysiologist Warren McCulloch of MIT as quoted in *Sleep* by Gay Gaer Luce and Julius Segal (New York: Coward, McCann & Geoghegan, 1966), pp. 274–275.

9. Ingmar Bergman as quoted in *Faith at Work* (February 1978), p. 18.

10. Arthur Koestler, *op. cit.,* p. 211.

11. Clark Pinnock, "Joyful Partisan of the Kingdom," *Sojourners* (December 1978), p. 26.

12. Thomas Merton, *Conjectures of a Guilty Bystander* (Garden City, New York: Doubleday, 1968), pp. 12–13. As quoted by *Sojourners* (December 1978), p. 4.

13. Robert Louis Stevenson, "The 'Little People' in an Author's Dreams," in *The New World of Dreams,* edited by Woods and Greenhouse, p. 51. This excerpt is from Stevenson's *Across the Plains.*

14. *Ibid.,* p. 54.

15. C. S. Lewis, *The Personal Heresy,* p. 119.

16. Roger Lancelyn Green and Walter Hooper, *C. S. Lewis: A Biography* (London: Collins, 1974), p. 181.

17. C. S. Lewis, in a September 15, 1930, letter to Arthur Greeves available in the Marion E. Wade Collection at Wheaton College in Wheaton, Illinois. Lewis called this "a very mortuary letter."

18. C. S. Lewis, in a December 20, 1943 letter to Arthur Greeves available in the Marion E. Wade Collection at Wheaton College in Wheaton, Illinois.

19. C. S. Lewis, *Poems* (New York: Harcourt, Brace & World, 1964), p. 81.

20. C. S. Lewis, *Letters of C. S. Lewis* (New York: Harcourt, Brace & World, 1966), p. 260.

21. William C. Dement, *Some Must Watch While Some Must Sleep* (San Francisco: The Portable Stanford, 1972), p. 98.

22. Synesius of Cyrene, "Dreams Take the Soul to 'The Superior Region' " in *The New World of Dreams* by Woods and Greenhouse, p. 160.

23. Sigmund Freud, *The Interpretation of Dreams,* p. 95. Freud is quoting from F. W. Hildebrandt's *Der Traum und seine Verwerthung für's Leben,* published in Leipzig in 1875.

TEN

THE GRACE
OF DREAMING:
OPEN HEARTS

*We need not, when a-bed, lie awake to talk with
God; He can visit us while we sleep and cause us to
hear his voice.*

John Bunyan, *Pilgrim's Progress*

Our Wildest Dreams

American writer William Dean Howells said that dreamers are
purely immoral. That tells us something about *his* dreams.

Henry David Thoreau was twenty years older than Howells and
must have led a stricter dream life. He said that in dreams we see
ourselves naked and acting out our real characters and that strong
virtue is ever wakeful and can order our dreams. The common
statement "I would never have *dreamed* of such a thing" reflects
the fact that we have moral authority over our dreams.

The following dream illustrates Thoreau's opinion exactly. Letha Scanzoni dreamed that a group of university students she

didn't know greeted her and invited her to come along up a hill with them. When she learned that they were urging her to go to a sex orgy, she told them that she couldn't join them, and they wondered why. She said, "This isn't my body!" That mystified them further, and so she explained that her body belonged first to Christ and second to her husband; she couldn't do anything with it that would displease either of them. The students understood and went on. Scanzoni's sleeping character is the same as her waking character. When there is sexual activity in her dreams, it is always within marriage to her husband. Scanzoni is a nonviolent person. She was deeply shocked once when, in a very bad dream, she sneaked up behind an evil Nazi guard and brained her with a rock because of her cruelty to all the Innocent prisoners. In another Nazi prison dream Letha preached the Bible to an evil guard instead of attacking, which is more true to character for her. My impression is that quite a few people lead full and rich but honestly circumspect dream lives.

My own dream life is quite innocent but not so virtuous as Scanzoni's. I have allowed a few married men in my church to get crushes on me, I'll admit. In each case some poor man is smitten with me and gazes at me fondly or gives me a quick kiss on the cheek at church. (These men would collapse with laughter in real life if they found out who they were.) One spring I dreamed that a particular elder was wild about me, and when I spotted his wife in the crowded church parking lot I knew she would hate the situation. A week or so later I dreamed that this wife had more or less adjusted herself to losing her husband to me and came to tell me with a worried look that she guessed the Bible said group marriages were all right. I said indignantly, "Oh, no! The Bible teaches strict monogamy!" I certainly wasn't going to share the man with her once I got him as my own legal husband. That wouldn't be moral! I was sorry to leave this woman out in the cold after she gave so many years to her marriage, but rules are rules.

About a month after that dream joke about self-righteously breaking up an elder's marriage, I allowed a different happily married man at church to develop sudden puppy-love for me, which he expressed by grinning at me with utter delight. Realiz-

ing, as I looked back at him, that this series of church flirtations
was not decent behavior, I thought briskly, "Well, I am just in a
phase in which I have affairs with other women's husbands, and
that's that!" It is clear now that some new outside interests were
helping me through some personal sorrows at that time in my life.
These outside interests were personified in my dreams as very
affectionate Christian men who wanted to make me happy. That's
that!

What about sexual dreams that are not so innocent? I had no
guilt about my sexual dream described in Chapter 8 because I
disowned that dream even before I learned whose it should have
been. The Greek philosopher Democritus, who developed the idea
of atoms about 400 B.C., suspected that our dreams come to us
from other people. If I suffered repetitions of that kind of thing,
I would try meditation, prayer, B vitamins, and even exorcism to
stop it. I suppose that such a problem is extremely rare or nonex-
istent, and surely most of our sexual dreams are our own fictions
not other people's facts.

Because it is natural for many people to experience sexual release in dreams, this excitement in itself is of little consequence.
These dreams may have meanings for us quite separate from
sexuality. For people who are really bothered by yielding to passions in their dreams, there are milder options than Origen's response to his lust, which was self-castration. First, one can plan
vividly and persistently to take charge morally or to have a helper
come into the dream to stop the seduction, using some variations
of Senoi methods. Second, one can turn the dream to good account
afterward by finding what the sexual contact can mean in deeper
terms, such as discovering and accepting a neglected aspect of the
personality, according to Gestalt and Senoi techniques.

I was amused to learn that in the Talmud there is reassurance
for Jewish men who worried about incest dreams. The Talmud
quoted the old sayings, "Call rationality Mother" and "Speak to
wisdom, 'You are my sister,' " and advised men to consider incest
dreams as uplifting symbols of union with reason and wisdom. I
would call that healing of dreams. People can transform an inappropriate sex partner in a dream to a symbol for any appropriate

strength or virtue and use the emotional energy of the dream excitement as a springboard for meditation about the good quality that came to mind.

An example of dream transformation is a dream I once had in which I went to see an outgoing female Christian writer, but my visit there was dominated by the sinister presence of a shadowy woman in the background. I tried to be gracious by saying, "I'm very glad to meet you, but I am even more glad to learn that you exist." It seemed the perfect thing to say, but I got no response, and then I awakened feeling rebuffed by both women. I decided the next day to go back to that room in my imagination, but I took the image of a trusted friend to stand by supportively during the encounter.

The most powerful figure in that dream was not the assertive writer but the shadowy woman. I asked her what she wanted of me, but she wouldn't answer. Next I tried asking her to take off her mask and show me who she really was, not knowing what if anything would happen. (I was working this out in the presence of my husband, who knows these techniques and made suggestions.) What should appear but a radiant, smiling, fairy-tale princess with a wand, who asked for my trust and wanted to give me a symbol to remember her by. It was quite clear that the busy writer was all along my conscious self and the shadowy partner of hers my unconscious (I prefer the term *hyperconscious*) self, waiting to be transformed to the image of what she is really like. She is, in this life, both the strange shadowy partner and the shining friend.

This means of transforming an unpleasant relationship in a dream into a memory that blesses in real life may very likely redeem some sex and violence dreams for people who are bothered by them. There isn't any danger of confusing this kind of dream work with outer facts of life or of going into a trance. Unlike a dreamer, a dream worker is completely rational, although the imagination is very independent and active. If the imagination ever tells us to believe or do something wrong in the course of dream work (mine never has), we can correct it.

Stéphane Mallarmé said that dreams have as much influence as actions, and he may have been right. But dreams have an extremely different influence from waking actions. Perhaps because of temperament or physiology some people seem to commit immoral acts in their dreams, but dream work is work toward moral health. Sex is probably the secret cause of much distrust of dreaming, but sex is not a good reason to distrust dreams.

If sex is one experience that really disturbs dreamers, death is another. Dream annals are full of true and false premonitions of death, visits from the dead, and perhaps a few postponements of death.

A French actor named Champmeslé dreamed in August 1701 that his deceased mother and wife were coming for him. He subsequently told his friends he was dying, arranged his funeral mass, attended it because he was still alive, walked outside to talk to friends who had attended his funeral, and dropped dead. A very recent similar story is told in *To the Ends of the Earth* by missionary writer Hugh Steven.[1] A healthy young Palikúr man in Brazil was told by an angelic figure in a dream that he would soon die. The next day he made things right with any villagers against whom he might have had negative feelings, and then he happily sang songs about God most of the night. The next day at work a tree fell on him, splitting his skull open. The dream had prepared him and his Christian friends.

Elizabeth Barrett Browning died in 1861. Two years later her sister Arabella dreamed that she was visited by Elizabeth and asked when she would join her. Elizabeth said, "Dearest, in five years." Arabella died four years and eleven months after the dream.

In 1945 Winston Churchill dreamed that he saw his dead body under a white sheet; his life was over. The next day he didn't die, but he did lose the election. The year when Churchill dreamed he died, a prisoner in a Nazi concentration camp dreamed that he would be set free on March 30. He believed it. When he was not set free on that day, he died on March 31. Victor Frankl, founder of logotherapy, was there and tells the tale in *Man's Search for Meaning.*

Dutch prisoner Betsie Ten Boom was extremely ill in a Nazi camp and foresaw that she and her sister Corrie would have a house for the healing of damaged people in Holland after the war.

She also saw that they would convert a concentration camp in Germany to a rehabilitation center. In her book *The Hiding Place* Corrie wrote, "She dozed fitfully during the day and night that followed, waking several times with the excitement of some new detail about our work in Holland or Germany."[2] Betsie said that by the first of the year she and Corrie would be out of prison. All of her prophecies came true; but Betsie's release came quickly through death, and Corrie's release to minister to the public came in life.

Stewart Alsop told a strange dream story in his *Newsweek* column of March 11, 1974. He had been suffering from a rare kind of leukemia with apparently fatal complications. An unidentified kind of pneumonia was finishing him, and the doctors had no way to fight it. He awakened, he thought, in his private railroad car (he was really in his hospital room) and announced officially, "We'll be stopping in Baltimore." He got up and staggered across the room, eventually opening the door and looking out at the station platform (the hospital corridor). He didn't like it at all. "We won't stop here," Alsop announced. "Start up the train, and carry on." As the train lurched forward, he managed to get back to bed.

The next day his lungs were slightly better, and to the amazement of the doctors his body healed itself of the pneumonia, allowing him several more months of life. He quoted with awe Shakespeare's well-worn statement in *Hamlet,* "There are more things in heaven and earth, Horatio, than are dreamt of in your philosophy."

"Perhaps my decision not to stop in Baltimore had nothing to do with my astonishing recovery," he concluded. "But there are mysteries, above all the mystery of the relationship of mind and body, that will never be explained, not by the most brilliant doctors, the wisest of scientists or philosophers."

Christian author Agnes Sanford has recounted in *Sealed Orders* how her husband Ted was healed of his fear of death by a dream. It was obvious that his heart could not last much longer, and, although he was a retired Episcopal priest, he greatly feared dying. One night he dreamed he was sitting in his favorite chair and found himself reviewing his life in various rooms of his, from boyhood to the present. He heard his doctor say he was dead, saw the clock point to midnight, and walked through the wall on a path of bright light. For the next five days he was happy and peaceful, and then he died suddenly in the chair he had dreamed he died in.

On June 28, 1914, at 4 A.M. the Bishop of Grosswarden dreamed he found a letter on his desk from his friend Archduke Franz Ferdinand, bordered in black like a funeral notice. When he opened the letter and read it, he saw the Archduke and his wife seated in a car in a crowd and then watched a man shoot them. At the same time the written letter said, "You Eminence, dear Dr. Lanyi, my wife and I have been victims of a political crime at Sarajevo. We commend ourselves to your prayers. Sarajevo. June 28, 1914. 4 A.M." Ten hours later the fateful murder occurred that triggered World War I.[3]

I have a friend who has told me only one strange story, and she has told it with conviction and consistency through the years. She has no particular interest in dreams except for this one. When Denise's first son was a new baby, his great-grandmother in another state was very eager to see him. One night the baby slept in a crib in his own room as usual, and his father sat up in bed reading as usual while Denise had already gone to sleep. She started laughing so much that her husband woke her up, and she said that she dreamed his grandmother was playing with the baby in a wonderful way. It had seemed very real. She went back to sleep and soon began to cry. He awakened her and she told him his grandmother wanted to take the baby away with her. She was so utterly terrified by the dream that they had to bring the baby in to sleep between them all night. The next day they got word that the great-grandmother had suddenly died just before Denise's two dreams.

Another acquaintance of mine has had many interesting dreams and tales to tell; this is one of her favorites. Her first husband had died young. When she was remarried and five months pregnant, she dreamed she was back at the funeral of her first husband, who sat up in his casket and talked to her. She had a curly-haired girl a year old with her, and he held the child fondly and said that she was very sick but she would be all right. Four months later Donna gave birth to a girl, and when she was one year old, with curly hair, she contracted a complicated illness. The doctor told Donna that the child's condition was serious, but Donna answered, "She'll be all right." She wondered why she said that; then she recalled her dream from sixteen months earlier. She did not worry about the illness, and the little girl did recover excellently.

Catherine Marshall has told of two dreams about Peter Marshall in *To Live Again.* About two weeks after his death she was having trouble believing that he was still alive. One morning, as birds awakened her, in a hypnapompic vision she heard him say, "Catherine, don't think of me as dead." It helped.

Later, after pleading with God for some knowledge of Peter's new condition, she had an extremely vivid dream in which she was briefly reunited with him. It was so convincing that she has always believed it was true and said so in her book. It seemed that she found Peter working in a rose garden and ran to his embrace, but she realized that Peter was somehow changed. Afterward God seemed to tell her that this was partial truth directly from his hand. She also had many confused dreams that "forgot" Peter had died and made her suffer her loss afresh when she awakened. She considered those painful dreams part of her need for emotional acceptance of her loss, in contrast to the dream that had been a revelation.

California minister Michael Esses has told in *Michael, Michael, Why Do You Hate Me?* that, one month after their toddler named Donnie was burned to death, Betty Esses was awakened by an intensely real dream of Donnie alive and well. She got up and prayed in her grief for a sign from God. She aimlessly turned on the television set and heard a minister's voice pray a prayer that seemed meant to fill her need. Then the unseen minister was identified as the family friend who had served as Donnie's godfather. Donnie was named after him. He had taped that prayer a year before Donnie was born, and it had been pulled out and played that night at random. Betty Esses felt that her dream and the old prayer had been arranged, and she was comforted.

One of the most touching and extraordinary dream accounts that I have ever read is in Virginia author Sheldon Vanauken's *A Severe Mercy.* First he mentions that the worst agony in his life as a young man was his repeated dreams of his beloved wife Davy dying. After her actual death a few years later he dreamed of her about once a month for over a year. All these dreams were joyful or a mixture of joy and pain. They were very emotional and important to him, but ordinary dreams.

Two years after her death, Vanauken dreamed that he was in Oxford again one bright, vivid morning, and that Davy appeared in his room. He knew that she was dead and believed that by some miracle of love God had allowed her to visit him. Davy claimed to believe the same. They hugged and laughed and talked, knowing she would have to leave soon, and he was pervaded with bliss. When she left by walking out the door, he thought, "How I have been blessed!" Then she appeared again for a moment to smile and wave, but now she was transparent instead of warm and solid. In his dream he knew what the basic difference was between these two kinds of manifestation, but he could never remember it later. Amazingly, the dream continued for a long time in great detail after Davy left. Vanauken has never had such a detailed, significant dream before or since. It left him with a serene, peaceful happiness that lasted a long time. He does not claim that Davy visited him, but he believes that on some level the dream contained truth.

Understandably, while writing this section I dreamed that I was with two of my friends who had never met in life. They both gave baby showers for my son ten years ago and both were mothers younger than I. In this dream the three of us were in a house across the street from mine that doesn't exist. I asked Rachel, who had become a growing girl again, how she could live after being murdered and buried. She said, "That wasn't me at all. That was someone else." She meant that the murder was no longer at all significant to her. I have many dreams of the dead, and I am usually aware that they have died. The dreams are often sad or wistful but never the slightest bit spooky.

I have had one dream that convinced me in my heart that I was visited by someone who loved me who had recently died. Like Vanauken and Marshall, I would not presume to interpret the level of truth in the event, but I treasure It beyond words. I think our society gives us the impression that this kind of experience is more rare than it really is.

Bishop Evodius once wrote to St. Augustine for advice on the subject. He had no question that such dream visits occur to Christians. He mentioned three friends by name, holy men, who had visited him after their deaths in dreams and told him things that came true. What he wondered was if our old friends and relatives really come to us in love as it seems or if a higher spirit assumes their form and visits our minds.

St. Augustine did not pretend to have a revelation from God about the matter, but he felt that dead people do not really come to us in our dreams any more than living people do. He felt that these apparent visits we have from them are angelic operations. His own background gave him a good reason to hold to that view. He had visited his own mother Monica in a dream once when he was still "dead in his sins." A young man asked her why she was crying, and she explained that her son was not a Christian. He told her to look at him, and she recognized him. From then on she had faith to go on praying and waiting for his conversion, which came in due course.

Encounters with Evil

C. G. Jung said that the conscious mind allows itself to be trained like a parrot and the unconscious does not, which is why St. Augustine thanked God he was not responsible for his dreams. He and many others have believed that we can be visited by fallen angels in our dreams. It is usual today to assume that negative spirits are projections from our unconscious mind rather than separate spiritual beings. (The Senoi have been credited with knowing that their dream "spirits" are really psychological; but they definitely believed in the separate reality of the spirits.) Evil spiritual beings were never disproved, of course; but they went out of style, although bad dreams continue. Bad dreams, whatever their source, are what scare many people away from looking into their dream lives for the nurture and blessing that is there.

Ironically, the first dream reported from an astronaut in outer space was called a nightmare. Gordon Cooper dreamed that he had failed to perform one of his essential tasks, one he had really accomplished already. Few of those interested in the details of Cooper's flight realized, probably, that the *mare* of nightmare comes from Old English *mara,* akin to German *mahr,* Polish *mora,* and probably descended from Sanskrit *mrnati,* he crushes. French for nightmare is *cauchemar,* pressing devil. Nightmares are crushing devil dreams.

Incidentally, the old word *succubus* can mean any demon or else a demon in female form that has sexual intercourse with sleeping men. The old word *incubus* can mean any nightmare or especially a demon in male form that has sexual intercourse with sleeping women. Henry Fuseli (1741–1825), an English artist from Zurich, Switzerland, became so obsessed with the idea of demons crouching on sleeping humans that he painted *The Nightmare* over and over with horrifying variations.

I have a mature Christian friend named Marty, a Bible student and teacher, who used to take what the Bible says about Satan and demons as symbolic of our imperfections. One night in a dream she had a personal encounter with evil that was so loathsome, so numinous, and so vile that she was shaken to the roots of her being. That was about ten years ago, and she recalls it as if it were yesterday. She could never have imagined such intensity of unmitigated evil. Strangely enough, this encounter was without form or setting of any kind; it was pure knowing. Aside from awakening her in utter terror and making her fear sleep for a few days, the dream did no harm. She assumes that God chose to give her an idea of what true evil is at heart so that she would not take it too lightly. She has personally believed in the reality of Satan ever since, although she doesn't stress it.

My most purely evil nightmare, too, was an apparent encounter with the worst of all spiritual evil. Mine was set at my own back door, where I stood as the evil being blew past me more terrible than all the hate, death, and atrocity in the world. I could still hear the almost swishing sound of its airy energy continue for several seconds after I awakened and knew I was safe in bed! The being, which I did not see, was like Tash in C. S. Lewis' Narnian Chronicles, but vastly worse. In no way do I consider that entity a projection of part of my unconscious. I think of it as the prince of the power of the air mentioned in Ephesians 2.

Once my husband had a dreadful dream in which he and a partner, both invisible, were dwelling secretly in a couple's home and violently assaulting them physically for no reason. I think they hit the poor people with crowbars, but of course the people did not know how they were being attacked. John was so revolted by his incomprehensible behavior and lack of identity in the dream that he told me about it. In my opinion it was a "Screwtape dream"—a demon's-eye view of demonic attack. It seems to disprove Diderot's rule that the one impossible dream is that the dreamer is someone else.[4]

I have had a few victim's views of demonic attacks in my dreams, two of which seem worth noting. In one my house was overrun with unknown boys who were smashing and damaging things. I was helpless, but I knew that if I could just call them by name I could force them to leave. This is obviously in the tradition of expelling demons by using their names. In a worse dream some evil ruffians were abusing us and threatening to kill John. In walked a friend of ours, Dale Godby, who was a graduate student in psychology at Fuller Seminary at the time. The ruffians, who had seemed all-powerful, stopped their cruelty immediately and said, "Blessings on you" to Dale. It is no coincidence, of course, that I take the name Godby to be an abbreviation of "God be with you" (like our word goodbye), and that something about Dale has often reminded me of Jesus.

Shakespeare expressed concern about bad dreams several times. In *King Richard III* he wrote:

O, I have passed a miserable night,
So full of ugly sights, of ghastly dreams,
That, as I am a Christian faithful man,
I would not spend another such a night
Though 'twere to buy a world of happy days.

In spite of the evil in them (whatever its source), I suspect that nightmares can usually be turned to good account. In the eleventh century the Bishop of Toul, who later became Pope Leo IX, dreamed that a horrible hag clung to him and tormented him. When he made the sign of the cross, she turned into an angel! Perhaps in a sense we can make the sign of the cross over our bad dreams afterward if we don't have them turned to good by a Dale Godby or an angel at the time. In the Talmud Rabbi Huna wrote that when you are disturbed by a dream you should tell the dream to three people who are willing to listen and to answer, "It is good and will remain good. God will turn it into good."[5] This reminds Christians of the famous fourteenth-century vision of Lady Julian of Norwich, in which Jesus assured her, "It is sooth that sin is cause of all this pain; but all shall be well, and all shall be well, and all manner of thing shall be well."

Christian author Jamie Buckingham, in *Risky Living: Keys to Inner Healing,* says that in 1968 he experienced what he calls baptism in the Holy Spirit and then began to relive many past sins of all kinds in his dreams. He suffered past immoralities and dishonesties and his mistreatment of other people. He consulted a minister who gave him some rather incongruous counsel: The Holy Spirit was dredging this up from his unconscious mind, and he should rebuke the bad dreams. In about two weeks the shameful series ended, and since then his dreams have become more spiritually meaningful than before. He claims that he sometimes hears God in his sleep.

John Wesley believed that some dreams are caused by bodily conditions, some from passions of the mind, some from good angels, and some from evil angels. I think these causes can be combined. Our son Peter had frequent night (and day) terrors for two or three years after he first saw the film *Dorothy and the Wizard of Oz* on television. Our pediatrician said that he has known of that particular film setting off that syndrome in several young children. The indescribable nightmares and waking hallucinations eventually seemed like demonic attacks or brief fits of mental illness. Finally we bought a big bottle of vitamin B-complex syrup for children and started to dose him with it. The night terrors stopped abruptly. They had been triggered by a psychological shock to a tender imagination, but they had been continued by an insufficiency of one of the B vitamins. Those dreams had been contributing all too much suffering to his otherwise happy life. To paraphrase a statement by Pascal, if a Nazi prisoner were to dream for twelve hours every night that he was a rich, free man, I believe he would be almost as happy as a rich, free man who should dream for twelve hours every night that he was a Nazi prisoner.

Author Lendon Smith, M.D., writes vividly about the role that falling blood sugar can play in producing nightmares. He notes that some foul people have sweet dreams, and some sweet people have foul dreams. One of his points is that falling blood sugar levels cause adrenaline to pour into the system, and this can create a sense of panic or doom. I know a woman who sometimes awakened in extreme panic an hour after going to sleep and was finally hospitalized one night, put on drugs, and sent to a psychiatrist. Although the psychiatrist was excellent, her night panics returned when she stopped the calming drugs. She finally had a glucose tolerance test and learned that hypoglycemia was the cause of the problem, the very syndrome described by Smith. He recommends that parents combat children's nightmares with relaxed evening talk about the child's activities, a hot bath, and a calcium and protein snack before bedtime. A sweet snack is, for some children and adults, the reason for bitter dreams.

Hardly anyone who has read C. S. Lewis' *The Voyage of the Dawn Treader* could ever forget the Dark Island, that place where every person's worst nightmare comes true. In that story Christ comes as a shining bird to lead the children out of the horror. The Bible passage that seems to me especially helpful when nightmares are a problem is Romans 8:38–39, "For I am sure that neither death, nor life, nor angels, nor principalities, nor things present, nor things to come, nor powers, nor height, nor depth, nor anything else in all creation, will be able to separate us from the love of God in Christ Jesus our Lord". (RSV). A hymn that I find assuring in answer to nightmares is "How Firm a Foundation":

How firm a foundation, ye saints of the Lord
Is laid for your faith in his excellent word.
What more can He say than to you He hath said,
To you who for refuge to Jesus have fled?

Fear not, I am with thee, O be not dismayed,
For I am thy God, I will still give thee aid;
I'll strengthen thee, help thee, and cause thee to stand,
Upheld by My righteous, omnipotent hand.

When through deep waters I call thee to go,
The rivers of sorrow shall not overflow;
For I shall be near thee, thy troubles to bless,
And sanctify to thee thy deepest distress.

When through fiery trials thy pathway shall lie,
My grace all sufficient shall be thy supply;
The flame shall not hurt thee; I only design
Thy dross to consume and thy gold to refine.

The soul that on Jesus hath leaned for repose,
I will not, I will not desert to his foes;
That soul though all hell should endeavor to shake,
I'll never, no, never, no, never forsake.

A Dream Within a Dream

For a person who lacks faith in a sustaining good nightmares can
be doubly sinister. Hamlet said it best:

To sleep: perchance to dream: ay, there's the rub;
For in that sleep of death what dreams may come. . . .

What if the nightmares of this life are only samples of eternal
reality?

From Socrates to Edgar Alan Poe, from Chuang Tzu to Bertrand
Russell, people have been wondering how to know that we are
awake rather than dreaming and wondering if after death we will
really awaken at last or, as Shakespeare suggested, go to another
phase of sleep and fearful dreams.

It is no wonder that some of us have mused as children along
with Poe:

Is all that I see or seem
But a dream within a dream?

A Dream within a Dream

Dreaming and then awakening into what is supposedly real life,
only to awaken again later from *that* dream is a fairly common
experience. It apparently delights some people and disturbs

others. Once I dreamed that I had an unexpected visitor, the world's foremost expert on *Peter Rabbit.* I felt ill and had to lie down for a brief rest before dinner. A stupid and unrealistic dream followed, which I observed as if it were a movie. When I awakened from it, I discovered to my horror that I had slept all night and half the next day and that my interesting guest had left unfed. I was so upset about oversleeping that I wept and wailed and awakened again and discovered that I had been taking an evening nap and had not overslept. I was sorry to realize that the *Peter Rabbit* expert had never existed.

One morning, still in bed, I told my husband that I had dreamed I was in Hawaii. (I have never been there and don't expect to go.) He asked, "Was that before we were married?" (We were married almost nineteen years.) I said, "No, it was even after we bought this house, and I dreamed it here." (We had lived in this house fifteen years.) Then I added, "In fact I dreamed it about an hour ago." As I realized that this is not our usual way of separating life into time periods, I began to suspect that I was still dreaming. That idea woke me up. I told my husband that I had dreamed I had told him I had dreamed I had gone to Hawaii. When I finished the whole story, he said, "Did you dream that before we were married?"

Another time I awakened in a hotel bed and knew that I was in my assigned room at a large conference. Then I awakened in another room and realized that the first awakening had been a dream. This kept happening. Only once was the room occupied by other people; I found that a fine singer I know named Dale Ziegler had been assigned to the same room as I and was entertaining guests there. When I awakened next in a private room I felt silly for having believed that I was to share a room with a male conference guest and was glad to be in the correct hotel room alone and wide awake. I soon awakened for the last time in my own bedroom. I wasn't at a conference after all! Freud claimed that a dream within a dream is always about key material we refuse to acknowledge. Some others have claimed that a dream within a dream is always key material we are featuring. I doubt both ideas because they use the word always.

I think my most interesting dream within a dream was when I

pulled into an underground parking lot with author Letha Scanzoni as my passenger because I needed to get something quickly in a department store. The lot was full, but I was determined and parked anyway and headed for the store entrance. A guard had a brief conversation with me about the parking situation. But as soon as he walked away, I heard Letha describing to my husband a very long, bizarre conversation I had just had with the guard in which I had actually jumped about like a dancer in my excitement. I realized that I had gone to sleep on my feet and dreamed a short simple conversation while really engaging in the long dialogue that Letha had witnessed. I stood there on the vivid oil-spotted concrete by the cars, looking at John and Letha and thinking that they did not know yet that I had just been in the most peculiar situation imaginable, the exact reverse of most dream delusions. My short simple dream had eclipsed a long, exciting actual event. I thought about how keenly awake and perceptive I was now after that strange dream experience. Then to my consternation I awakened and found myself at home in bed.

As I explored the meanings of that dream, the first thing that popped into my head was the pun, "There is a lot below the surface!" It went on from there. It was a good dream and a tricky one. As I write about it, I don't have the slightest doubt that I am now awake. But I have, in fact, done lots of other writing and typing in my sleep in the mistaken belief that I was awake. Bertrand Russell, hard-headed philosopher and mathematician, remarked once that he did not believe that he was dreaming but he could not prove that he was not. That admission is in a great tradition. Plato recorded a dialogue of Socrates with Theaetetus in which the two decided that there is some doubt about whether we are awake or in a dream, no matter how sure we are of our own wakefulness.

If life in this world is a dream of some kind, the next question is, Who is the dreamer? As a young child I used to secretly wonder if I might be only a part of someone else's dream. I decided it was more likely that I was the dreamer, and then I used to worry about the reality of the world around me in case I should awaken. Later I decided that, if this is anyone's dream, it must be God's.

Lewis Carroll played with this idea mercilessly in *Through the*

Looking Glass. In Alice's dream Tweedledum and Tweedledee informed her that the Red King, whom she saw sleeping, was having a dream about her and that if he were to awaken she would go out like a candle. When Alice threatened to awaken the King, they informed her that she couldn't do it, being only a thing in a dream. When she wept with frustration and claimed that being able to cry proved that she was real, Tweedledum replied with contempt, "I hope you don't suppose those are *real* tears?"

Here Carroll seems to me to be spoofing Descartes' "I think, therefore I am" with "I hope you don't suppose those are *real* thoughts?"

In a later chapter with the ambiguous title "It's My Own Invention" Lewis Carroll himself appears in his own book as the foolish but kindly White Knight. Alice wonders how he can go on talking quietly when he has fallen on his head into a ditch, and he answers with surprise, "What does it matter where my body happens to be? My mind goes on working all the same. In fact, the more head downwards I am, the more I keep inventing new things." Carroll claimed to have invented this story in a dreamy state. At the beginning of this chapter Alice decided tentatively, "So I wasn't dreaming, after all . . . unless we're all part of the same dream. Only I hope it's *my* dream, and not the Red King's! I don't like belonging to another person's dream."

Years later Carl Jung himself had what I call a "Red King dream." He saw a yogi meditating in a chapel and awoke with fright at the thought, "He has a dream, and I am it."[6]

On a recent dream trip to England, I asked my English friend Ian to tell me if I was really awake or just dreaming, and if I was dreaming to please awaken me. I explained that I was so happy to be with him that I suspected I must be dreaming, but I figured I must be awake because I had already experienced twenty-four hours in England as well as all the preparation for the trip and the trip itself. As I elaborated upon the trip, I became less coherent and ended up talking sincerely about how I had been driving every day and night. When I finished, Ian said drily that he would wake me up, but he didn't want to bother to do it right then. Such an odd response made me suspicious that he was dreaming also. Neither one of us would be apt to talk this way awake. My big question then was, "Are we here together in the same dream or here together in different dreams?" I awakened before I had a chance to ask Ian his opinion. He went out like a candle in my dream; perhaps I went out like a candle in his. We have dreamed about each other many times.

The Way

This dream reminds me of Taoism, which is at the heart of C. S. Lewis' *The Abolition of Man*. As Max Zeller said in *The Dream: The Vision of the Night*, "It is difficult to define the concept of Tao and to penetrate its complexity in a few words. . . . It is translated as 'the way,' or 'meaning,' or 'path.' The Jesuits called it God."[7] In Chinese writing the word *Tao* is composed of the characters for consciousness (head) and for following a path (going). Together the signs imply going consciously forward to a goal. It is the way of faith and intuitive morality.

I think that, when I told Ian that I keep traveling every day and night, I was revealing the experience of the right hemisphere of the brain, the unsleeping night driver, the path follower expressed in the Tao. This "going" experience is memorably pictured in George MacDonald's *The Princess and the Goblins,* in which the princess has an invisible thread to follow that leads one aright. "But, remember, it may seem to you a very roundabout way indeed, and you must not doubt the thread."[8] W. H. Auden said that MacDonald's finest gift as an author was his "dream realism, his exact and profound knowledge of dream causality, dream logic, dream morality."[9] The magic thread and the Tao are followed by faith.

If the path-following aspect of the Tao seems to be reflected in the right hemisphere of the brain, the consciousness aspect of the Tao seems to be reflected in the left hemisphere of the brain. This possible correspondence to human physiology in no way negates the Tao as the living path and, for believers, God himself.

Lao Tzu, the founder of Taoism, wrote of it:

The Way itself is like some thing
Seen in a dream, elusive, evading one.
In it are images, elusive, evading one.
In it are things like shadows in twilight.

In it are essences, subtle but real,
Embedded in truth.

Robert Ellwood, in *Many People, Many Faiths: An Introduction to the Religious Life of Mankind,* explains that in Taoism ordinary rational waking consciousness is not the measure of all things. Taoism's first and greatest explainer, Chuang-Tzu, liked to shake his readers loose from the ordinary way of seeing things. That is why he told them that once he dreamed he was a butterfly, and when he awoke he did not know if he was Chuang-Tzu who had dreamed he was a butterfly, or a butterfly dreaming he was Chuang-Tzu. "The dream world, in other words, is just as real as any other. . . . The world of the unconscious and the imagination, he is saying, is just as much a manifestation of the Tao as the rational—and may indeed better lead us to comprehending the Tao."[10]

In Christian terms, the dream life may help us to comprehend God. It may be half the journey of the soul.

Victor Frankl says in *The Unconscious God,* "There is a way by which the unconscious—including its spiritual aspect—yields itself to exploration, namely, by way of dreams. . . . Our goal is to lift not only instinctual but also spiritual phenomena into consciousness—and into responsibleness."[11] One of his patients was asked to share a dream with Frankl's group. She told of finding herself in a great crowd of people who were all going one direction while she struggled to go the opposite way. She was trying to move toward a light she saw in the heavens. The light grew brighter and brighter and condensed into a figure. That was all she had to say.

The group pressed her to describe the figure, and she refused as long as she could. Then she murmured, "The figure was Christ." Although he is not, perhaps, a Christian himself, Frankl said the message to his patient is unquestionable.

In *Beyond Ourselves* Catherine Marshall described how Jesus came to the hate-filled criminal Starr Daily in a dream when he was in solitary confinement and very ill. He knew "I am submerged in Reality, I'll never be the same again, now and through all eternity."[12] He awakened an absolutely new man, found eventual healing and release, and became a good friend of Peter Marshall.

Morton Kelsey tells of his own less outwardly dramatic change of direction from ordinary secular orientation to real spiritual orientation: "... the consideration of dreams brought my own religious faith and practice to life."[13]

Kelsey was already a "Christian" when his dreams made it real to him. The Basuto of Africa, who were being evangelized in the early decades of this century, usually waited for an indication in their dreams after they felt consciously ready to become Christians. Once a dream indicated that their souls turned to Christ, then they would be baptized.

More recently a Palikúr witch doctor in northern Brazil had rejected the Christian message, perceptively replying, "I work to get spirits *out* of people. Why do you speak of letting God put his Spirit *into* them? I do not want to be under God's control." After a severe beating from his angry and bitter young wife, the witch doctor knew he was gradually dying. He had visions of demons coming to get him and told the whole village he wished he had come to God through Jesus, but he was convinced it was too late. No one could change his mind. Fortunately, he had a dream in which he saw a large book with the names of all the village Christians written in it. His, of course, was not there. In his dream, he asked God to write his name in the book. After that he told people before he died that he was joyful to be lifted up by Jesus. This story is related in Hugh Steven's book *To the Ends of the Earth.*[14]

I know a missionary who had much more ordinary guidance from a dream. Felicia dreamed that she and her young daughter were traveling third class on an interisland ship in the Philippines and that the repulsive food on the ship was too dirty and old for her to eat or to feed the child. The dream was upsetting. When she asked herself what it was in her waking life that she couldn't stomach, she realized that she was deeply disturbed by the lack of privacy in the family's housing. As a result of her dream, they moved. It was well worth the effort.

Felicia is a Bible translator and would be surprised at some of my Bible translations in my dreams, I suspect. Twice that I know of, for example, I have updated the imagery in Matthew 7:3–5 in the Sermon on the Mount, which warns us not to try to take a speck out of someone's eye if we have a log in our own. Once in a 1975 dream a mother brought me her son, who had had an eye accident. I held his damaged contact lens in my hand and felt its surprising heat; a hot contact, I mused. Then I explained to his mother that, although I went through many years of medical school to become a doctor (I thought it strange that I couldn't remember going to medical school at all, but I figured that since I was a doctor I must have gone to one), I was not an ophthalmologist. In fact, I said, I didn't take care of my own eyes and contact lenses; I went to a specialist as her son should do.

My next dream on that subject took place in 1978. I dreamed I was removing lens after lens from my left eye. I realized that I had carelessly accumulated many defective old lenses there through the years, most of them dark or deformed. I assume that this symbolized getting rid of old views. For the rest of my life I will respond more emotionally to Matthew 7:5 because I can't imagine taking a log from my eye, but now I can imagine taking a pile of defective lenses from my eye. Shortly after that dream I found my left contact lens unbearably painful one morning and discovered that it had been chipped in its case during the night and looked like some in my dream. I went to a new shop for the first time to get it replaced and learned that my old shop had made my right lens stronger than the prescription called for. This accounted for eyestrain and visual trouble I had been suffering several months, wrongly attributed to my age. Here I happily added interpretation of life to interpretation of dreams and felt encouraged to reject strong corrections from people who supposedly know their business, if the corrections don't meet my true needs.

I had a vastly more profound dream about Matthew 7 many years ago and completely missed the meaning until recently. I simply saw a frantic, neurotic woman, some kind of shrew. I said "What is wrong with her?" and The Voice answered, "She won't do what she should do." The impact of that statement woke me up, because I suddenly knew the woman was a caricature of myself. I worried about that dream because I felt that, although I was no shrew, it was very important. I didn't know how to deal with dreams then. There were hard problems in almost every part of my life that I was battling with all my might. In spite of serious health difficulties I carried an extremely heavy load of church work and tried to serve others day and night. I drove myself. When it seemed I could do no more, I did even more. Physically and financially I did it with less and less. Yet the dream said, "She won't do what she should do," and so I kept straining. I felt I should hear and respond to every kind of appeal that came my way, and I felt distraught about all the appeals I simply had to refuse. I was an overachiever if there ever was one, yet I knew I did not respond adequately to the dream judgment. I was sorry I ever had the dream. It hurt.

The seeming uselessness of that shrew dream reminds me of a recent dream in which I was returning a blouse to Sears after storing it in my closet a long time. I decided I had no use for it and would donate it to their thrift shop. The clerk who was handling the return looked the blouse up in an old Sears catalog and read its glowing, detailed description to me. "That's a wonderful blouse," I replied. "I'm going to keep it and wear it after all." I knew without a doubt that this was a comment upon unused dreams that eventually become valuable to their owner when rightly interpreted.

Very recently I looked at the old dream about the neurotic woman again, which had been "stored in the closet" all these years. "She won't do what she should do," The Voice had said. So now I said simply, "Well, what *should* she do?"

"Ask," The Voice replied kindly.

"Oh my," I answered.

Well, I might as well see the joke in it, as I'm sure God does. You have not because you ask not, Jesus said. I never got the message of the dream until I asked for it.

In Matthew 7:6 Jesus warns us not to give dogs what is holy. In Gestalt terms I had given a holy dream to my "inner top dog" and let him use it against me for years. (My personal fault is not laziness but taking on too much.) The dream had been, all along, pointing me back to Matthew 7:7, "Ask, and it will be given you; seek, and you will find; knock, and it will be opened to you"

(RSV). I know where my basic life lesson lies. I suppose that, at this rate, in another ten or fifteen years I'll start to learn it better.

The following scriptural application to my life is perhaps my favorite. I dreamed I was on a narrow, crowded beach looking desperately for my missing sons. The sea was choppy and dangerous. The life guards were playing games. Suddenly a strange dark creature, shiny wet, arose from the surf about twenty yards away. It was something like a hippo and an elephant in looks and size. It arose, immobile, above the water on the back of a similar beast that was larger. This one arose on the back of a larger one. The fourth one stood there in the water, the size of a house, at the base of the living tower. The spiritual power of the animals was overwhelming; they were mute, terrible, and wonderful. Suddenly I was in a fine store and my sons greeted me with kisses—both of them radiantly neat, clean, healthy, and happy. (At that point I should have realized this had to be a dream.) In my utter joy I started to buy them handsome new shirts and take them out for special food as a celebration.

I awakened, sorry to have it end, and tried to figure out what this was about. I could tell right off that the crowded sand was my outer life, and the choppy water was my inner life. It then came to me that the four creatures were life elements in a certain New Testament passage that I did not recall well. I went back to sleep.

The next morning I located the passage I was looking for in Romans 5:3–5 by using my concordance. Suffering produces endurance, endurance produces character, character produces hope, and hope stands firm. In fact, as I see it, hope supports character, character supports endurance, and endurance supports suffering. Best of all, hope ls fulfilled in that God's love is poured into our hearts through the Holy Spirit given to us. What more vivid illustration of that love for me than my dream reunion with my children and gifts for them!

This kind of illustrated version of Romans 5:3–5 is in no way Bible scholarship. It is, I think, the Spirit's way of making that Bible passage part of my own heart knowledge through extremely potent personal imagery. If I ever get any sense, I'll meditate upon that entire dream vision more often and perhaps avoid being preoccupied by every new emergence of suffering—which is only the first beast in the story. The Talmud teaches that some dreams come to us to remind us of important guidelines. I believe it.

By My Soul

Once I lost my husband rather than my children. This occurred in a dream on September 22, 1972. John was on a ferry that sank in a flood. I was on a hill surveying all that happened with growing terror. I told a nice man there how worried I was. John had been tired looking, the last I saw him, in a brown suit. There were many survivors and no report of casualties, but John was nowhere in sight. The man told me he could see John; he did not tell me where. He said for me to sit down and watch and I would soon see him, and then he left me there. I wondered what he meant. I sat and waited a bit, still afraid, and then I awakened. I turned over, and there was John in bed by me. My heart swelled with relief and joy. The man in my dream still seemed real to me. "Is this what he had in mind?" I wondered. Of course. And suddenly I knew who he was. The Spirit of Christ had appeared as an ordinary man.

Morton Kelsey suggests at the end of *Dreams: A Way To Listen to God* that the dreamer within is the Holy Spirit. Feeling cautious, I am not ready to attribute all dreams to the Holy Spirit. I would guess that we spend some dream time in routine pursuits that don't amount to much, as we do in waking life. But I certainly believe that the Holy Spirit plays a large role in our dream life and can turn any humble dream into a blessing.

On October 20, 1976, I dreamed I was washing a carrot at my kitchen sink. (I always suffer some degree of pain standing there, so washing carrots is not a pleasure to me.) As I placed the carrot on the counter to my right, a hand took it from me, touching my hand. I was filled with supernatural warmth and joy, which lingered after I awakened. That had to be the touch of Christ, to my way of thinking. The dream needed no interpretation in order to bless me, but I think the idea that came is correct. This was a picture of the fact that Christ is "working with me."

My friend Esther had a new license plate on her not-new car

that meant a lot to her. In California people can order special numbers or letters on their plates by paying extra, and Esther had splurged and used her girlhood name, E TRUE. I was with her the afternoon in 1978 when she went to her car and discovered that a plate was missing. She assumed it was stolen, but it may have come loose somehow. She was distressed because of the time and money that it would cost to replace the plate; she keeps very busy and frugal as a leading volunteer Laubach literacy teacher, Sunday school teacher to little children, and mother and grandmother. She looked for the lost plate a bit in vain.

That night Esther dreamed that she and a man went looking for her lost sign that said TRUE, up and down the dim, empty streets of south Santa Ana. She never wondered who her friend and helper was. They would cover areas separately and meet at chosen intersections. They seemed to look for hours. Finally when they met the last time, the man told Esther she could go home. He had found the missing plate and propped it up on her front porch for her.

Esther's husband George, a high school science teacher, awakened her soon with the good news that he had just found her lost license plate propped up on the front porch by someone. "Who would have brought it so early in the morning? Who knew it was ours?" he wondered. "Why didn't they ring the bell?"

George and Esther never learned those answers. None of their neighbors knew a thing about it. Whatever happened or didn't happen on her front porch, Esther is positive about who her dream helper really was. I agree with her. I think this was another "Road to Emmaus" dream. There are famous old stories of Christ appearing to Constantine and St. Martin of Tours in their dreams. I guess he could appear to a loving woman named Esther Brown.

It makes perfect sense for a nonbeliever to see these dreams as wishes or projections and for a believer to see them that way or as the presence of angels that remind us of Christ. One of my own dreams predisposes me to see the figure as the Spirit of Christ himself.

At the end of 1975 I dreamed that I walked into the home of a neighbor I had in my childhood to throw away some trash I was carrying. I thought the place was rented now by a certain retired widow of that neighborhood (who, to her surprise, moved in there in 1978, never hearing of my dream). Instead, I found the wise young woman who lived there in my childhood; I apoligized sincerely for not knocking and told her my problem. She gracious-ly referred me to her husband, Ralph, whom I have known mainly as a father and teacher in real life. He led me, with my trash, out to the apartment building in his back yard (where he was not just father and teacher but landlord) and looked for his big trash barrels in the garage of that building for me to use. I saw a very small box there. I suddenly realized that all the trash I had was a tiny ball of paper inside my fist—a crumpled note of some kind. So I put it into the landlord's little box and thanked him over and over for his help.

When I thought about this funny dream later, feeling that there was a mystery in it, I thought, "Let's see, Ralph's last name is Davidson. Son of David." Instantly I was sobbing my heart out without knowing why. Later I realized what the dream had meant. In it Jesus had enabled me to let go of an intense grief I carry. I know better now what the priesthood of Jesus means. I know what must have been written on the note. I don't belong to a liturgical, confessional church. I go back to that garage in my mind sometimes with Jesus and throw away the same little ball of paper again. I cry again. I'll probably do it all my life. It is better than carrying the paper in my clenched fist.

I think that many people have dreams of the triumphant return of Christ and of being in heaven. They are unforgettable experi-ences that influence our lives and need no comment. When they come they can't be missed.

All these extraordinary Christian dream experiences remind me of a dream I had in 1974, in which I found myself exploring an absolutely gigantic, rambling church building, as I have often done in dreams. This time I came to a meeting in one room on the ground level attended by a close friend of ours, Bob, who is a logical engineer and active Christian. The event was posted as an "anti-charismatic meeting" and was to feature a "Western ensem-ble" for entertainment. (I have tried on a fancy "Western ensem-ble" in a clothing store in a dream since then and decided not to buy it.) I declined the meeting, thinking that it might be just right for Bob but not for me. I went on exploring, going deeper and deeper down many stairways. I did not feel quite safe. I suspect that something I feared at the deep levels was the buried pain that I encountered in my later dream about Davidson and the crumpled note. I'm glad I kept going.

Another haunting dream I had took place at a rummage sale. Among all the odds and ends of worthless junk I saw a figure of an Egyptian princess in full regalia. The more I looked at her with appreciation, the more lifelike she became. She opened her eyes once or twice. Then she sat up and talked to me in perfect English! She was beautiful. She told me that her ancient civilization was so advanced that they could travel to our place to get things to take back with them. She seemed to indicate that they liked to learn things from me. I knew that what the wise Egyptians could learn from me was basic Christian truth. When I considered this lovely dream later, I came to the peculiar conclusion that my conscious self has the privilege of teaching my "unconscious" self Christian truth, even during the dream process in which the unconscious is more active. Among the apparent junk in dreams there can be a special quality of contact between two inner worlds. This dream sent me back to Romans 12:2, which tells us not to be conformed to our outer world but to be transformed by the renewal of our minds. Both my self that I know and the "unconscious" Egyptian-princess part of my mind need renewal. Both hemispheres of the world belong to God; both hemispheres of the brain belong to him. That's my conviction.

Another beautiful woman came once in another dream. I had to spend a day on errands for someone. It would leave me tired and farther behind in my own work, which was already too much for me. I had a sour attitude for twenty-four hours before the time came, and my attempts to see the situation in perspective failed totally. I was very resentful and frustrated. During the errands I had a chance to doze in my car for a moment, and I saw a lovely woman's face. If there was more to the dream, I couldn't tell. But my heart was light from that moment on, all day. "It's all right!" I thought.

Another of my loveliest dreams came in 1976. I was on my kitchen porch and saw Habesch, my dear cat that had disappeared

a couple of years earlier along with many other cats in our neighborhood. It was obvious that someone had killed them all at once.
Now I called him and he came right to me, still looking healthy
and beautiful. I decided that this was absolutely impossible and
that I was dreaming, but I didn't wake up. Furthermore, everything was utterly, concretely real in every detail, although I was
looking intently for flaws or vagueness. All was solid, intact, and
normal. After awhile I looked up at lovely clouds shining pinkly
in the late afternoon sky. They were correctly lighted from the
west. I purposely allowed myself to see great people walking on
them, roseate like the clouds. It was beautiful beyond description
and must have been a glimpse of heaven. I said wistfully, "One
can never see people walking on the clouds where I live," and
awakened.

The most important dream I ever had about heaven was only
a glimpse from the outside. In 1974 I dreamed that I was in a group
that was following directions about heaven in this life. We were
doing a routine like walking in a circle and tossing crowns into the
center, lifting hands and singing. I thought it was all right, but not
very beautiful or interesting. I glanced to the side, and for a
moment I saw a wall made out of cubes of some kind of crystal,
and on the other side of the wall the reality that corresponded to
our little practice was taking place in ultimate beauty and joy. The
reality in heaven was absolutely unlike our little exercises, yet
they corresponded; and ours was caught up in the other and
magnified it. Everything there is became clear to me, and I was
flooded and overwhelmed with joy. Of course this shock awakened me, and the supernatural perceptions I had been given were
gone immediately.

All I had left was the crude, fragmentary idea that our clumsy
attempts at praise in this life play a real part in a dance of light
and meaning that is going on so vibrantly beyond the wall that
it is a wonder we are not knocked down by a hint of the rhythm
of it and blinded by a split beam of its reflected light and struck
mute by the slightest vibration of the meaning. I had doubted the
transcendent value of our clumsy human praise of God before that
dream, feeling that we do it for our own edification and discipline.
I thought worship was tame until then. It is perhaps more lIke

tipping over perpetual tidal waves of love when we pour out once a thimbleful of trying to care. One awkward, passing human kindness may echo as an eternal tumult of joy.

Someone will say, Well, she was only dreaming. Right, and now I am only waking. The word *waking* comes to us from the Indo-European word for vigor and is very closely related to *vigil, watch,* and *wait.* There is nothing more basic to the word *awake* than keeping guard. For what are we really watching and waiting and keeping guard? Life, I think, and more life.

In contrast, our word *dream* comes from the Middle English *dreme,* probably from Old English *dream,* which meant joy and music. It is akin to the Old Norse *draumr,* German *traum,* Medieval Dutch *droem, drome,* and *droom,* and the Old Saxon *drom.* It is especially closely related to the Old Frisian word *dram.* These all mean dream, but the last also means (shout of) joy. I think of the dream of joy in Psalm 63, a song of David:

Your love is better than life itself,
my lips will recite your praise;
all my life I will bless you,
in your name lift up my hands;
my soul will feast most richly,
on my lips a song of joy and, in my mouth, praise.

On my bed I think of you,
I meditate on you all night long,
for you have always helped me.
I sing for joy in the shadow of your wings;
my soul clings close to you,
your right hand supports me.

Psalm 63:3–8, The Jerusalem Blble

Notes

1. Hugh Steven, *To the Ends of the Earth* (Chapaqua, New York: Christian Herald Press, 1978), pp. 41–42.
2. Corrie Ten Boom, *The Hiding Place* (Carmel, New York: Guideposts Associates, 1971), p. 196.

3. Herbert Greenhouse, "The Dream That Triggered World War I," in *The New World of Dreaming* by Woods and Greenhouse, pp. 87–88.

4. *The Encyclopedia of Philosophy,* Volume 2, p. 401.

5. Sandor Lorand, "Dream Interpretation in the Talmud," in *The New World of Dreams* by Woods and Greenhouse, p. 155.

6. Carl Jung, *Memories, Dreams and Reflections* (New York: Vintage Books, 1961), p. 323.

7. Max Zeller, *The Dream-The Vision of the Night* (Los Angeles: Analytical Psychology Club of Los Angeles, 1975), p. 150.

8. George MacDonald, *The Princess and the Goblin* (Philadelphia: David McKay, 1920), p. 131.

9. W. H. Auden, "Introduction," in *The Visionary Novels of George MacDonald* edited by Anne Fremantle (New York: Noonday Press, 1954), p. vii.

10. Robert Ellwood, *Many Peoples, Many Faiths* (Englewood Cliffs, New Jersey: Prentice-Hall, 1976), pp. 169–170.

11. Victor Frankl, *The Unconscious God* (New York: Simon and Schuster, 1948), p. 40.

12. Catherine Marshall, *Beyond Ourselves* (New York: McGraw Hill, 1961), p. 244.

13. Morton Kelsey, *op. cit.,* vii.

14. Hugh Steven, *op. cit.,* pp. 45–48.

EPILOGUE

Homer: A dream is from God. (*Iliad*)

Aeschylus: The mind asleep hath clear vision. (*Eumenides*)

Clement: Thus also such dreams as are true, in the view of him who reflects rightly, are the thoughts of a sober soul, undistracted for the time by the affectations of the body, and counselling with itself in the best manner ... (*The Instructor*)

Origen: ... that in a dream certain persons may have certain things pointed out to them to do, is an event of frequent occurrence to many individuals ... (*Against Celsus*)

Tertullian: Now who is such a stranger to human experience as not sometimes to have perceived some truth in dreams? (*A Treatise on the Soul*)

Rabbi Jonathan: The man is shown in the dream what he thinks in his heart. (*The Talmud*)

Fra Giovanni: The gloom of the world is but a shadow. Behind it, yet within our reach is Joy. There is radiance and glory in the darkness, could we but see, and to see we have only to look. I beseech you to look. (1513)

Sir Thomas Browne: We are somewhat more than ourselves in sleep and the Slumber of the Body seems to be but the Waking of the Soul. ("Of Dreams" in *The Works of Sir Thomas Browne*)

Russian Proverb: We are shrewder at sunrise than at moonrise.

Goethe: Man cannot persist long in a conscious state; he must throw himself back into the unconscious, for his root lives there. (As quoted by Arthur Koestler in *The Act of Creation*)

There have been times in my life when I fell asleep with tears in my eyes, but in my dreams the most delightful visions came to me to comfort and cheer me, and the next morning I would rise again feeling fresh and happy. (As quoted by Norman MacKenzie in *Dreams and Dreaming*)

Lewis Carroll: "Dear, dear! How queer everything is today! And yesterday things went on just as usual. I wonder if I've been changed in the night? Let me think: *was* I the same when I got up this morning? I almost think I can remember feeling a little different." (*Alice's Adventures in Wonderland*)

Edward Von Hartman: I may be proud of the work of consciousness, as my own deed, the fruit of my own hard labour; the fruit of the Unconscious is as it were a gift of the gods, and man is only its favored messenger; it can therefore only teach humility. (*Philosophy of the Unconscious*)

Ralph Waldo Emerson: A skillful man reads his dreams for self-knowledge . . . However monstrous and grotesque their apparitions, they have a substantial truth. ("Demonology" in *Lectures and Biographical Sketches*)

Henry David Thoreau: Dreams are the touchstones of our characters. (*A Week on the Concord and Merrimack Rivers*)

George Macdonald: I believe that, if there be a living, conscious love at the heart of the universe, the mind, in the quiescence of its consciousness in sleep, comes into a less disturbed contact with its origin, the heart of the creation; whence gifted with calmness and strength for itself, it grows able to impart comfort and restoration to the weary frame. (*Wilfred Cumbermede*)

I think in order to convey to us the spiritual help we need, it is sometimes—just as according to the psalmist, "He giveth to his beloved in their sleep"—to cast us into a sort of mental quiescence, that the noise of the winds and waters of the questioning intellect and roused feelings may not interfere with the impression the master would make upon our being. (*Weighed and Wanting*)

William James: But just as our primary wide-awake consciousness throws open our senses to the touch of things material, so it is logically conceivable that *if there be* higher spiritual agencies that can directly touch us, the psychological condition of their doing so *might be* our possession of a subconscious region which alone should yield access to them. The hubbub of the waking life might close a door which in the dreamy subliminal might remain ajar or open. (*Varieties of Religious Experience*)

Helen Keller: I like to think that in dreams we catch glimpses of a life larger than our own. (*The World I Live In*)

G. K. Chesterton: One can find no meanings in a jungle of skepticism; but the man will find more and more meanings who walks through a forest of doctrine and design. Here everything has a story tied to its tail, like the tools or pictures in my father's house; for it is my father's house. (*Orthodoxy*)

Sundar Singh: The brain is a very delicate and sensitive tool, fitted with many fine faculties which, in meditation, can receive messages from the unseen world, and thoughts which go far beyond normal human consciousness. The brain does not work up these thoughts; they come to it from the spiritual world, and the mind translates them into a language which is suitable for human circumstances and situations. Many people receive such messages in dreams ... (*The Gospel of Sadhu Sundar Singh*)

Rufus Moseley: If the Lord can't make me listen any other way, He sometimes talks to me in dreams. (As recalled by Agnes Sanford in *Sealed Orders*)

Carl Jung: If a theologian really believes in God, by what authority does he suggest that God is unable to speak through dreams? (*Man and his Symbols*)

W. H. Auden: Every normal human being is interested in two kinds of worlds: the Primary, everyday, world which he knows through his senses, and a Secondary world or worlds which he not only can create in his imagination, but also cannot stop himself creating. ("Afterword" for *The Golden Key* by George MacDonald)

Howard Thurman: It is the nature of dreams to run riot, never to wish to contain themselves within limitations that are fixed. Sometimes they seem to be the cry of the heart for the boundless and the unexplained. Often they are fashioned out of longings too vital to die, out of hankerings fed by hidden springs in the dark places of the spirit. (*The Inner Journey*)

Eric Fromm: The paradoxical fact that we are not only less reasonable and less decent in our dreams but that we are also more intelligent, wiser, and capable of better judgment when we are asleep than when we are awake. (*The Forgotten Language*)

Paul Tournier: I am well aware myself of how ... the analysis of a dream reveals to me unconscious guilty propensities which can then be humbly confessed and by God's grace forgiven ... I may add that dreams, as many examples in the Bible show, may often appear to be messages from God. A child once remarked to his mother: "Dreams are God's movies, aren't they?" (*The Person Reborn*)

John Sanford: In deallng with thousands of dreams I have not yet found a single aimless or meaningless one. (*Dreams: God's Forgotten Language*)

Max Zeller: In "A Midsummer Night's Dream" Shakespeare speaks of the "airy nothingness" that surrounds us in dreams and imagination. Yet this "airy nothingness" is hardest reality. It influences the direction of life and determines its course, if and when we perceive it. (*The Dream—The Vision of the Night*)

Morton Kelsey: As I began to take an interest in my dreams, I became aware for the first time in my life that God wanted to speak to me. (*Dreams: A Way to Listen to God*)

Theodore Roszak: If I were to suggest that in your dreams miracles of self-discovery have taken place, that in the ocean bottoms of sleep you have found your way to sacred ground ... you would be incapable of verifying or refuting the suggestion. (*Where the Wasteland Ends*)

Mary Patricia Sexton, CSJ: The only way to personhood is inward. (*The Dante-Jung Correspondence*)

Catherine Marshall: In the years ahead I believe there will be exciting experimentation on this subject among Christians. God will lead us through our dreams to all sorts of provocative discoveries about our hidden selves in His plan to refashion us into whole people. (*Something More*)

INDEX